Praise for *Awakening Stories*

"Rumi states, '*God sleeps in the minerals, dreams in the plants, moves in the animals, and awakens in man.*' In this process Unconditional Love embodies ITSELF, creating conditions so that each being—each of us—can be *loved unconditionally.* Like an infant awakening from the dream of itself to the conscious realization of its "self," we swim in the river of life . . . sometimes drowning, sometimes battered on the rocks, sometimes saved. *Awakening Stories* will inspire you, no matter how battered on the rocks you may be, to seek the light of your soul and be the light for others, for in the darkness, *light is always born.*"

— Paul Chek, Founder, Chek Institute

"How many people in the world are satisfied and truly happy to be living on this planet earth? The state of our planet is the reflection of the state of humans. Water is the mirror of our hearts. The world we are seeing right now is the reflection of the collective consciousness. As water stores and carries the information, it's time for us to heal the water on the earth so that the world will be in peaceful vibrations. To heal the water, we humans need to heal ourselves first. When humans are free from traumas, from fear, the world will be a peaceful and harmonious place. I know that the powerful stories in this book will reach many people around the world so they are healed and begin to bring peace on earth."

— Michiko Hayashi, Ambassador of the Emoto Peace Project

"I found these stories to be delightful and would recommend this book!"

— Anita Moorjani, *New York Times* best-selling author of *Dying to Be Me, Sensitive Is the New Strong, What If This Is Heaven?,* and *Love: A Story About Who You Truly Are*

"*Awakening Stories* uplifts and inspires through first-hand, personal transformational experiences occurring in apocalyptic times. Indigenous civilizations such as the Hopi inform us that the world has ended a few times before, and we are currently crossing from the fourth to the fifth world. We can benefit in such times by learning from the heartfelt stories of those who are thriving after undergoing the reconstructive experience of awakening consciousness. The promised Golden Age of Shambhala is here right now, and *Awakening Stories* beautifully illuminates the way."

— Cynthia Sue Larson, author of *Quantum Jumps, Reality Shifts,* and *The Mandela Effect and its Society: Awakening from ME to WE*

"These captivating stories will activate deep inner wisdom and truth in your heart and soul. *Awakening Stories* will shed light on any places that need healing and reconnection with the warmth, peace, love, and joy of who we really are. This collection of inspiring stories will bring you to the center of your loving place in the cosmos, simultaneously coming home to yourself and a sense of oneness with everything."

— Emmy Vadnais, Intuitive Healer, Health Coach, and CoHost of the *New Thinking Allowed* YouTube channel with Jeffrey Mishlove, PhD; author of *Intuitive Development: How to Trust Your Inner Knowing for Guidance with Relationships, Health, and Spirituality*

"*Awakening Stories* opens up the doors to understanding that awakening experiences are as varied and unique as those who experience them. There is no "one-size-fits-all." It also offers a solace for readers who may be searching as they find insights and understanding that resonate with them in the pages here. *Awakening Stories* is an invitation to explore deeper and also feel the common human experience of consciousness expansion as we move into our collective awakening."

— Debra Moffitt, award-winning author & intuitive

"Become immersed in the stories of individual Awakening. Such varied tales of finding 'One's Truth,' inspiring the Soul to hold on to the KNOWING that for each and every one, there lies within us the opportunity to 'find home.' We all walk our own pathway, each gaining insight and experience along our journey. Yet, ultimately, when LOVE—TRUE LOVE—awakens within us, our Hearts are never the same. *Awakening Stories* is filled with many beautiful 'Soul Stories' from those who are willing to share their journey in order to uplift. Thank you to Each One."

— Blossom Goodchild, direct voice channeler and author

Awakening Stories

Awakening Stories

Edited by Allison Brown, EdD

Palm and Lotus Publishing

Published by Palm and Lotus Publishing

www.palmandlotus.com

ISBN: 979-8-9851252-9-0

Contents

Introduction

The world as we know it—as we have always known it—is in the throes of an increasingly rapid and profound change, an evolutionary shift, the likes of which we have never experienced. This is not a new concept. Eschatology, the study of the end of the world or "end times," is a feature of all major religions, indigenous cultures worldwide, and even doomsday cults. Typically, it takes shape as a grand showdown between good and evil . . . an *apocalypse* . . . that changes the course of history. Indeed, this great shift has been prophesied for thousands of years.

The Hopi have spoken of intense social and ecological disruption that will eventually lead to a new era of lasting peace. The "end times" predictions of the Abrahamic religions generally include a period of tribulation—marked by increasingly severe, man-made and natural disasters—culminating in world peace, upon the Second-Coming of Christ. The Dharmic religions tend to speak of this era in terms of decay, redemption, and rebirth.

In the context of mysticism, an *apocalypse* is viewed a bit differently. Yes, it still implies an ending. However, it is the deconstruction itself

—the end—that allows for new growth and evolution. We witness this pattern within all of nature: the circle of life, a spiral of birth, death, and rebirth. All living things exist in a state of constant renewal, and it is only within the decomposition that we can view the potential. It is the indomitable spirit of nature, of humanity, to push forward, to grow, to create something new from the ashes, as the phoenix from the flame.

We understand that, within the struggle and pain of adversity, lie the nuggets of wisdom and the seeds of growth. A baby chick must, alone, break free from its shell in order to fortify the strength to survive on the outside. Similarly, the experiences that challenge us, as humans, often uncover a hidden power within . . . one that may also provide us with fresh perspectives and unexpected opportunities. Just as a butterfly emerges from its cocoon a new creature, we, too, resurface from our trials anew, frequently unrecognizable . . . the old being left behind.

So it is, as well, with Earth and the human collective. We are, together, entering a time of new beginnings, but it will not be without struggle. We are crossing a threshold of no return. Indeed, what we are leaving behind can no longer be accessed . . . can no longer *exist*. Humanity is evolving into what some are calling a New Earth, a new *reality*, one in which humanity realizes and dwells in the divine, where we begin to recreate the structures of our world from a foundation of Love. And so, the *apocalypse*, the collapse of the old is essential. The old ways of being are no longer working and will no longer be supported.

This chaos will not only take place on a global level; we may also experience turmoil within our individual lives, as well, shaking us out of complacency and forcing us out of our comfort zones. The internal crisis might take the form of a divorce, job loss, illness, or the death of a loved one. Our struggle might be triggered from the stress of the external chaos—war, social unrest, or political instability. Again, this is purposeful. This *pressure* is how each of us will create the New Earth within Self.

Take heart, however. As Carl Jung understood, within chaos, there is a secret order. Within chaos, there is opportunity . . . there is hope. The plan for our New Earth has been divinely orchestrated and is being divinely guided. There is beauty and peace on the horizon. In fact, there is beauty and peace NOW, if we are willing to see it. Each of us, whether we realize it or not, is contributing to the energy of this collective transformation. Our physicality might be operating on auto-pilot, but our consciousness understands what is happening and is *excited*, because we are awakening into wholeness . . . into the truth of who we are as divine Beings. We are starting to realize that we are part of something much grander than our own individual lives.

As this internal shift takes place—this *awakening*—our awareness begins to expand, bringing forth new understandings, new ways of being, and even new "gifts." You see, this New Earth operates within a higher level of frequency or vibration; therefore, humans will be able to access Beings, energies, and abilities that function from this higher dimensional plane of existence. What was previously invisible will become visible; what was unclear will be revealed. These revelations might include messages from a deceased family member, episodes of telepathic communication, or instances of unmistakable inner guidance. As our vibration increases (a byproduct of this awakening process), our path becomes clear; without effort, the perfect people and circumstances show up at just the right time.

In the chapters that follow, twenty-three souls—ranging in age from twenty-six to seventy-three—magnificently recount their personal awakening journeys. The paths they describe span a variety of compelling and universal themes within humanity: trauma, religious deconstruction, nature, betrayal, death, divorce, animals, addiction, illness, and much more. Our anthology authors allowed themselves to be, in many cases, quite vulnerable, as they share the story of their transformation from pain to healing, bondage to freedom, grief to joy.

Within these stories, you will recognize yourself. No two awakening journeys are exactly the same, to be sure; each of us is on our own unique, divinely-guided path. But as a member of this human collective, we find pieces of ourselves within the experiences of another. We *feel* this shared humanity as we witness a mother holding her newborn, a firefighter carrying a child to safety, or a soldier returning from combat. And it is through these universal, human experiences that we will find our way home . . . back to ourselves and the divinity within.

—Allison Brown, EdD

Chapter 1
Homesick
Julie Sivell, MDiv

I think I was born homesick. As long as I can remember, I've felt a recurrent longing for something I couldn't find or place. Something inside of me seeks a sign, a signal, an impulse, a feeling or a knowledge that I'm home and I belong. Even when I am physically at home, as soon as the distractions clear, there it is, in the hollow of my belly, in the back of my mind: homesick. It's a strange thing to be born a human being on planet Earth. In the best of circumstances, we grow in this beautiful womb space with all of our needs met until we are thrust out into the world completely vulnerable and dependent on other human beings who may or may not give a rip. Luckily for me, my parents were/are loving human beings who did care.

When I was born three months early in 1974, my mother and I were placed in two different hospitals. I needed NICU and an incubator, she needed to recover from the surgery required to have me. She was told to rest and not to drive a car for six months, but she left the hospital as soon as she could walk to drive her car to sit by my incubator, poking her pinkie finger into the top of the cube every day until they let her bring me home. Daddy paced the halls until the few minutes every day when they'd let him hold me. Analytical people might say being placed in an incubator, lacking touch and hugs and a home for my first several weeks on Earth caused a need in me. Could be. But when I think of that incubator—its stillness, its warmth, the soft light, the low hum of oxygen—I feel safe and cared for. Turns out, being alone doesn't make me nearly as homesick as being with other people can.

So what does it mean to feel "at home?" Is it a place we can build? Is it a simple matter of buying a house, filling it up with stuff you like and then feeling safe within it? I've done that a few times. I've moved into places I liked, homes I was excited to inhabit, and after the busy-ness of moving wears off, there it is again . . . that feeling. Homesick. If it isn't a space, then surely it is the people in the space who create a home.

My truly good and loving parents divorced when I was five years old. Weekends became a shuffle between houses and families. Worlds began to separate, and what was "our family" became "Dad's family" or "Mom's family." So I moved between worlds; re-attenuating to the different spaces and faces, reacquainting myself with the relation-ships in this world or that world, as needed. I have to say, I knew then and now that my relatives loved me, and there was very little contention or friction in all of this. It's only that I became a satellite, circling around, but never quite knowing where the center was. When I was with Mom, I missed Dad. When I was with Dad, I missed Mom. The feeling of longing continued and grew as I grew, and so I looked around for comfort.

Music and books were the ballasts I carried with me from house to house. Both of my parents had record players or radios on all the time and it was easy enough for me to carry a book with me back and forth. Melodies and fictional characters have been the antidote for loneliness for lots of people. My mind would much prefer to jump into the setting of a book, read about the characters and imagine their world rather than live within my own. Real people require so much more than fictional ones. A fictional character asks nothing but to be observed and followed along with. It's a common experience to be in the middle of a conversation with someone and feel lonely, but I rarely, if ever, feel lonely when I am listening to a good song or reading a book. Yet, music and books can only help you so much. Eventually, we want someone to ask about our day, how we are, and we seek a deeper connection.

Looking for connections typically consists of interacting with external stimuli and trying to find meaning and "ourselves" within it. Most of us have tried it all: exercise groups, alcohol, church, drugs, therapy, social media. Scrolling, scrolling, scrolling for something or anything to remind us that we are not alone, that we belong. We are tribal creatures and media companies capitalize on our need for community through endless loops of images and jarring headlines. BUY THIS TO FEEL BETTER. DRINK THIS TO BE THE TYPE OF PERSON YOU WANT TO BE. YOU ARE GOING TO DIE FROM (insert disease here) UNLESS YOU TAKE THIS (insert remedy here). We scurry from car to building, from app to app, from screen to screen, looking for safety and a place we can rest and feel at home. A sense of belonging and familiarity become even more elusive as we clutch at everything we can see and buy to try to create it.

Maybe the answer lay somewhere deeper, I thought, so I turned away from the external and focused on the spiritual. I had gotten a bachelor's degree by this time, switching from the University of Southern California to the University of Georgia and my major from print journalism to religion. Straddling worlds, per usual, I had one foot in popular culture and one foot in something deeper. I liked the antiquity of the study of religion; the ancient languages, the anthropology of it, the study of cultures and meaning.

One continuity in my childhood had been going to church every Sunday, which I recalled as a very peaceful, nurturing experience. So when I found myself divorced with a two-year old, I turned to this study again and pursued a Master of Divinity at Wake Forest University. Hebrew, Aramaic, Greek and Latin became daily discourse along with history and the impact of religion on past and present society. The music I listened to had typically given voice to the rebellious, angry and alternative. Now, studying at Wake Forest, I was learning about other disenfranchised populations and how they had been left out of mainstream religion throughout history. It seems there have always been these wild voices at the fringes of societies, warning us to stop trusting the government, to pay attention to our relationships, to care about each other or to cut through the bullshit. Turns out that Jesus Christ and Kurt Cobain weren't that different and neither was their message of inclusion and truth.

Somehow, this labor of learning caused the opposite of understanding. The more I studied and learned, the more I focused on separations. Little did I know, the more we fixate on our separateness from one another, the more miserable we become. Still, looking through history, one can't ignore that majority groups dismiss the needs of the most vulnerable populations in society, at best, or exploit them, at worst, and how the needs of the "widow" and "the orphan" are very rarely truly met by church communities despite performative overtures.

Century after century, religion has been a mechanism used to funnel money from everyday people, maintaining power for the cruel, using guilt and fear to control the vulnerable. Religion was a game, a con, a system designed, like all other systems, to keep us in check, keep us coloring inside the lines, a way to offload any critical thinking or personal responsibility. If God existed, He was either a megalomaniac psychopath or somewhere distantly outside this realm of war, fear, control and abuse.

After three years, I graduated. Thesis written, judgements firmly in check, heart hardened, I knew it all. My professors assigned a scripture to each graduate and they gifted me with, "And you will seek Me and find Me, when you search for Me with your whole heart" (Jeremiah 19:13). Somehow, in my search for God, I found a whole lot of ego. The "Me" I found was extremely human.

Self-righteousness is a wonderful protective mechanism. The feeling of homesickness was replaced by a feeling of superiority. I was doing great. Instead of searching for a deep mystical meaning or absolution from a divine Being I could not see, I was free to be whoever I really was and dictate my own days rather than be a victim to this overwhelming search for meaning. I could handle this little reality of mine. Until . . . I hit a crisis. Life-changing crisis rips through the pieces of our crafted lives, and we either fall spectacularly apart or somehow, back together.

I was thirty-five years old when my mom died of cancer, untethering me from my sense of home again and causing me to seek support. My self-righteousness was shown to be a hollow friend, indeed. Books and music weren't cutting it. Nothing seemed to lead me out of the cauldron of grief, but I had two small children and a husband who needed me to function, so checking out was not an option either. I made an appointment with a former therapist who had lost his son and seemed to have effectively navigated the experience of grief, himself. My therapist was beginning a new group, gathering clients with the intention for each of us to explore connection to others. We met every Wednesday evening and honored the specific instruction to, "stay in the room," meaning that we could not wander when talking. We had to stay mentally present and only discuss what was happening in the room. Sounds easy, right?

When you get present and stay present, you can no longer use blame as a cloak. For example, there is no pointing your finger to any outside circumstance insisting, "He caused the problem" or "That experience caused my actions." When there is silence, you must stay with it and not jump to a comforting excuse you've used about your dog, daughter, parents, job, coworker or whatever. Stay in the room.

The longer I stayed in the room, the more apparent it became that each member in these sessions was reflecting me back to myself. At first, I could just find points of connection, empathy, understanding, as we got to know one another. Over time, this understanding deepened. One night, our therapist tasked us with going around the room and using one emotional adjective to describe each member of the room. Each individual would use one word to describe the emotional state of the person whose turn it was. For example, when it was Bill's turn, each person in our group said a feeling word out loud, in turn. We heard, "sad," "lost," "happy," "determined," as we went around the nine members of the group. Well, when it was my turn in the hot seat, every member of this group used the same word to describe me.

"Angry." "Angry." "Angry." "Angry."

Nine times.

I was astonished. And I couldn't even blame anyone or anything outside the room! I couldn't use my mother's recent death or my husband's shortcomings or my selfish in-laws or any of my usual trump cards. I couldn't explain that I'm a really nice person, it's just all these *things* kept happening to me. The charge of this group was that I had to hear it, sit with it and eventually acknowledge this reflection of myself being placed right in my face. What a gift. To be confronted with yourself in a space you trust with no easy way to hide or prevaricate—this was work—the most meaningful, precious kind of work.

I had to stop outsourcing my identity to music, books, religion and circumstances and get real. Homesickness hit once again. It was time to get to the bottom of it, and the only way I knew how to do that was to ask questions. I had to keep drilling down within every interaction to start to understand the differences and similarities between me and you, me and others, me and the world, on and on. What was the difference between perception and reality, if there even was one? If my perception didn't align with another person's reality, what was going on there? If we all agree that there is no one definitive way to do any certain thing, then isn't any way okay as long as it functions? And who decides whether it functions or not? I kept asking questions, in my mind, over and over, until the truth would reveal itself under the layers of other people and systemic ideas and training. I started to understand that to react against something is the same mechanism as conforming to it. Whether you are obedient or rebellious, you are still being controlled and defined by the force you react to. I wanted to understand who I am beneath any action or reaction. I searched with all my heart.

Years of asking questions and staying in the room, waiting for answers, has brought me deep understanding but nearly as often, more questions. At the core of those questions is the central one: what am I homesick for? I think about this one as I walk through my day, continue to construct a life in 3-D, running errands, going to work, doing laundry. There are moments I feel at home, moments where I feel genuinely connected to my life and those around me; usually when I am in nature or speaking one-on-one with a loved one. My dog is one of my great teachers. She seems fully present in each moment and every little thing is The. Best. Thing. Ever. My husband likes to say, "The present is a present," and I try to stay in it, unwrapping it, accepting it as it is, appreciating it without careening to the past or future in some mad, anxious effort to protect myself from risk or imaginary harm. All is well in the present, if you choose to accept it. When I accept the moment, there is no separation, no homesickness.

One woman I learned about in divinity school was Julian of Norwich. My father's name is Julian, I am Julie, and we named my daughter Julian after my father and as a tribute to Julian of Norwich.

Her *Revelations of Divine Love*, written in the fourteenth century, after the Black Death plague, expresses deep, deep contemplation of the mystery of life, God, and the resounding love she feels in response to her questions.

> *And in this he showed me a little thing, the quantity of a hazelnut, lying in the palm of my hand, it seemed, and it was as round as any ball. I looked thereupon with the eye of my understanding, and I thought, 'What may this be?' And it was answered generally thus: 'It is all that is made.' I wondered how it could last, for I thought it might suddenly fall to nothing for little cause. And I was answered in my understanding: 'It lasts and ever shall, for God loves it; and so every-thing has its beginning by the love of God.' In this little thing I saw three properties; the first is that God made it; the second is that God loves it; and the third is that God keeps it.*[1]

I could choose to dismiss this religious statement or the religious text simply because it was written in a church by a woman who surely, at that time, did not practice social justice or blanket equality. But I feel a deep resounding peace within Julian's words as she contemplates a hazelnut. I can choose to either shut my mind to it, dismissing it, or I can accept my earnest reaction to it. I choose to accept the peace arising from words written over six hundred years ago and bring that sense of wonder into my present moment. "What am I?" or, in Julian's diction, *"What may I be?"* And the answer is, I am "all that is made . . . lasting and ever shall, for God loves [me] and so everything has its beginning by the love of God." This is not an exclusionary statement but a radical love including Every Single Thing we can see or contemplate. What a holy idea. Wholly holy, if you will. There is nothing outside of all that is made.

Homesickness is the un-remembering of the love of all that is made,

---

1. Julian of Norwich, *Revelations of Divine Love*, chapter V "Westminster Cathedral Treasury, MS 4"

all that was created, all that is. I awaken to the reality that there is no "me" to be found, no "home" I lack. By my very existence, I am the same as all that was made, all that is, all that will be. And so are you. We've heard the statement, "Home is where the heart is." I've dismissed it as too trite, too simple. But that could be because we imagine this as a home full of people we love. The problem in this concept is that home, in this configuration, will always be missing someone. Rarely is everyone we love in the same place, under the same roof. Yet, home *is* where the heart is when you reside inside your own heart space.

When we look outside at external things, people, relationships to fill us up or to be our home, we will inevitably feel homesick. No thing or person can do that for us. It's our responsibility to connect back to ourselves and release the separateness. Just as group therapy taught me that every person reflects a part of me back to myself, loneliness or homesickness lets me know that I have temporarily forgotten to connect back to myself, my heart, me. *Remember*, my heart reminds me, *you are all that is made*. Everything I see and experience is a part of me. I can never be separated from it. Home is not a place from which I am exiled. It is not a place to be, a Being to be, a group to join. Home is me. I am home.

What do I do with this? When I connect with others, either through conversation or writing, I help them sweep away the stories they are buying or selling about themselves in order to get to their true, authentic Self. Every tale we build about our separateness, our division from Self or others is simply that: a story. What is infinitely more interesting to me and of utmost value to all of us, is the true Self residing underneath all of the stories. It is my calling to remind you of your own unique signal emanating from and to yourself. In each interaction, I am listening and feeling out for your true signal so that I can acknowledge it and support its resonance in our world. Our particular signals issue out through the universe via words, thoughts, and sounds, frequencies that are wholly our own but can find harmony with other frequencies when they join without drowning them out. Words, like people, are individual sounds or ideas which, when combined with others, create entirely deeper meanings, rarely canceling each other out. How utterly amazing.

Julie Sivell is a dedicated educator currently serving as the English Language Arts Teacher and Department Chair at St. James Santee Middle School, where she teaches sixth to eighth grade. Julie's initiatives include founding a book club, implementing a "Reading Buddies" program, and organizing educational field trips, such as a visit to the International African American Museum and a storytelling-focused trip to Universal Studios. Her creative and independent approach fosters a positive and engaging learning environment with a focus on improving fluency, comprehension and writing skills.

Julie's expertise extends beyond the classroom. As the Communication and Development Coordinator for The Sophia Institute, she worked with the National Institutes of Health (NIH) under the White House to draft a social justice initiative for Charleston's racial healing plan. She owned and operated American English Editors, providing editing services for multi-language learners, including PhD dissertations and academic journal articles.

Julie holds a Master of Divinity from Wake Forest University and a TESOL certification from Columbus State University. She earned her Bachelor of Arts in Religion/Print Journalism from the University of Georgia. Her dedication to education and literacy has been recognized with several grants and awards, including the Bright Ideas Grant and Bosch Grant, and she is a board member of the South Carolina Association for Middle Level Education (SCAMLE).

Married to her husband, Anthony, and mother to Sam and June, she still returns to books and music daily. In her spare time, she can be found helping high schoolers work on their college admissions essays or walking her dog. She continues to search for the meaning of life, the necessity of the Oxford comma, and the best cup of coffee.

For written musings or otherwise, contact Julie at jsivell@aol.com.

Chapter 2
When Life Gives You Lemons, Demand to See Life's Manager
Evan Brown

When you don't know anything, you think you know everything. At least I sure did. But who doesn't think they know how the world works when they are a kid? It's a part of growing up. To understand the end, you have to start at the beginning. At least, that's what they say . . . but I have never been one for tradition, so let's start in the middle. The next question is, the middle of what, exactly? To say that the journey is over would be to say that there is nothing more to learn or nothing more to experience, which just can't be the case. Having lived only a quarter century at this point, there simply has not been enough time of me existing on this earth for any one journey to truly be complete, so how can anyone put an endpoint on your story? How do you go about marking key milestones and quantifying the impacts of certain events throughout your life? If time moves forward without regard for the past, how can past events shape the future? The story of one's spiritual enlightenment isn't a clean-cut linear notion; it's an under-construction roundabout with skid marks and potholes.

My relationship with religion has always been an interesting thing. As a kid, my parents, being from a religious background, would drag my sister and me to church with them every Sunday. Naturally, this was met with reluctance and dismay from two kids who just wanted to watch the Sunday morning cartoons. Although I never became a convert, I did have a respect for people who did—they believed in something greater than themselves, and to me, that seemed like a reasonable prospect. Where I took issue, of course, was when someone would expect me to blindly follow something, just because they were the one leading the way. As we grew up, my parents started to question that same thing, and as time went on, we gradually stopped doing the whole organized religion thing in lieu of other avenues yet to be revealed.

Growing up, I engaged in all the typical kid stuff: played sports, attended summer camp, discounted school, ate junk food, and watched too much television. I also did plenty of atypical kid stuff, like worry about the family finances and question authority. I hardly had the care-free childhood experience; I was riddled with anxiety and worry all throughout my childhood. My supportive and loving parents did everything they could to assist me and allow me to thrive. The problem was that I did not have any interest in much, as the idea of trying something outside of my comfort zone was a fate worse than death. I wanted nothing more than to curl up at home and become a hermit.

As time went on, things got more controllable, and I started to branch out a bit in high school. I credit the biggest shift in my mentality as the *semi-coerced* decision to join the Army National Guard my junior year of high school. This forced my hand to start finding ways to control my anxiety and taught me about structure and resiliency. Hindsight being what it is, this was the kick that my life needed to push me over the edge from a worried little kid to a confident young adult. It was during my senior year of high school, however, that we would take a family vacation that would completely change my perspective forever.

I Like Big Buddha's and I Cannot Lie

"Hawaii or a cruise?" That was the choice given to my sister and me for what would be our 2016 spring break vacation. It wasn't much of a decision, really. A cruise to the same locations we've been to before, compared to the opportunity to go someplace new and cool? That choice was posed to us months in advance; still being in the flurry of high school, our itinerary during the trip meant nothing to me at the time. It was just another family vacation. So off we went, on what would become the most transformative trip of my life.

Fast forwarding to about halfway through our weeklong trip, the plan for the day was to drive around the island of Oahu and visit the Byodo-In Temple and Polynesian Cultural Center. I should add that, at the time, I was more worried about how I was going to stay entertained on the drive around the island than what it meant to visit these amazingly significant sites. Being a passive observer of my parents' awakening journeys, I had a very loose touchstone to what all of this spiritual mumbo-jumbo was about. But like any other teenager, I didn't want anything to do with that.

Throughout our childhood, my sister and I were always well traveled. As kids, my parents used what would have been a traditional 'college fund' to subsidize our summer vacations to places like Europe, Scandinavia, and Central America. As a kid, I never had an appreciation for what we did or where we went, at the time. But looking back, I am eternally grateful, as it opened up my eyes to different cultures around the world. Before the Hawaii trip, we had been to several historically significant sites across Europe, and we were always taught to respect the history and culture of the places we traveled. Why should this one temple on a random island in the middle of the Pacific be any different? How was I supposed to know that my whole life was about to be turned upside down?

So there I was, standing at the base of a ten-foot tall, golden Buddha statue in this sacred temple, as the walls of my life started to crumple in around me. I was suddenly alone in this world, falling into the swirling black hole beneath me. As my grip on reality weakened, all I could do was listen helplessly to the ceremonial bell being struck outside the temple, the seams of my universe tearing open with every strike. It was as if the hand of Buddha himself reached down and plucked me off of this earth. There was no fear, no anger, no confusion. There was only pure emotion and connection to a power beyond my own. In that instant, my soul was lifted out of my physical body and allowed to breathe for the first time.

As I started my descent back to Earth, all I remember is my whole world spinning around me as I stumbled out of the temple, trying to maintain my composure while also trying to comprehend what was happening. My parents had helped me over to a bench where all I could do was sit and cry, as I listened to them try to explain what I had experienced. It must have been an hour before I was able to compose myself enough to walk back to the car, but it would be another few days until I was back to my 'normal' Self. It wouldn't be for years to come that I would be able to truly understand what had happened that day, but what I *did* know is that what had happened was very real and launched me on my path to spiritual enlightenment.

Are We Not Going to Talk About the Ghost in the Room?

How can anyone expect to navigate an ocean of uncertainty alone? We all need a good teacher to guide us along our path, and I have been extremely lucky to be guided by many people throughout my journey, both physical and spiritual. These guides flow in and out of my life as I need them, but there are certain constants that will forever remain fixed to my journey. Until you start to listen to what your guides have to say, you will never progress through your journey. When the ghosts in the closet start speaking to you, take a listen . . . they might be onto something.

After Hawaii, I started down the typical path of those trying to understand their place in the universe. This path was guided by my parents, who at the time had only just started their own journeys of spiritual awakening. Casting the widest net I could, I spent time with mediums, friends, and practitioners in the spiritual world, trying to glean experiences from every angle of understanding. As with everything in my life, I did not fit neatly into one niche or subscribe to every aspect of the traditional approach to spirituality. Gaining a base of knowledge in the fundamental aspects of controlling certain types of energy and understanding how it flows through our universe allowed me to carve my own path and begin my own journey.

Some of the biggest support I received during that time came in the form of different spirit guides and a late friend who came to me during meditation. They let me in on a little secret that, no matter where I was in life, they would be with me to share their love and support. Learning how to channel that energy into progressing my journey would be *my* burden to bear, however. It would not come until much later that I would finally figure out how to tap into that energy stream, and for that understanding, we have to take a trip to the Appalachian Mountains.

Listen to the Roar of the Mountains

To talk about my journey of spiritual enlightenment without discussing my connection with nature would be doing a great disservice to one of the very core identities that I hold near and dear to my heart. From an outside perspective, most people would say that I just have an expensive hobby and that I take too many trips into the mountains . . . and they would be right, for the most part. If you were to tell the young version of myself that we would be spending weeks and months at a time, outside, hiking mountains, he would flat out not believe you. But what is to some people just a weekend hobby is a vital part of what helps me refine my spiritual connection in my life.

There are quantifiable health benefits to being out in nature, so why couldn't there be spiritual benefits that go along with it? When I first started hiking alone, I was constantly on edge, always scared of getting lost or getting stuck in bad weather. Now, while those are certainly valid concerns that every new hobbyist has until they gain experience, in my case, I received spiritual reassurance before I gained what could be considered the appropriate amount of experience. As I broadened my understanding of spiritual connections at home, I would bring those connections with me into the outdoors. I knew that no matter where I went, my spirit guides were hitching a ride.

The mountains are like a tuning fork. They allow me to fine tune my connection with whatever spiritual energy I need at that time. For me, being in the mountains was more than just a physical connection to nature; it is a connection to all time and energy, past and future. There are moments when I stand on the tallest peak or climb the highest hill that I can hear and feel the energy flow that connects us all. When you are surrounded by that kind of raw energy, it can be intoxicating in the way that it cleanses your need for physical wants or desires.

The first time I experienced this type of true spiritual connection was during a several weeks-long backpacking trip in northern Virginia. I had set off to hike south along the Appalachian Trail from Harper's Ferry, West Virginia to Waynesboro, Virginia, a distance of about 160 miles. I would be spending roughly two weeks hiking that distance, and it would be only my second multi-week trip of the sort. Starting off that trip with an unshakable feeling of unease and lots of anxiety, as I was still new to long distance backpacking, I had a very long and unenjoyable first day on trail. My plan for the first night was to hike to a Potomac Appalachian Trail Club-owned trail center called the Blacksburg Trail Center, where I could camp for the night.

After arriving at the trail center, I was surprised to find that there were only one or two other people there, and I was greeted by the camp host, a younger girl named Moxie. While making dinner around the picnic tables, Moxie invited me to join her on a nightly trip up to the top of a nearby summit to watch the sunset, which I, of course, gladly accepted. Thinking it would be a good way to clear my head and get a good view, we set off up the trail . . . a short hike, with her dog and little brother in tow. Once at the summit, we made ourselves comfortable, while we waited for the sun to drop. She and I lightly chatted about our experiences on trail, her brother playing with the dog, next to us. Because she was spending her season as caretaker learning how to play the violin, Moxie asked me if it wouldn't be a bother if she took this time to practice. As I sat on top of that mountain overlooking the Shenandoah valley, watching the sun set, every pull of her bow string was like a knife slowly sawing away at the only tether I had left holding me onto the earth. When that rope finally snapped, I felt myself leap away, caught by the energy currents of the mountains like a leaf in the wind.

It was at that moment that all of my worries had been carried away. My need for control over my physical presence was released, and I was able to coast freely along the lazy river of spiritual connection. Then came the emotions. All of my pent-up emotional pressure suddenly released like shackles being taken off; I was set free. The remainder of the night was a blur, but for the rest of the trip and for the rest of my life, I would have an unspoken, unbreakable connection with the energy that surrounds us and connects us all . . . so long as I give up what control I think I have and let the energy guide me to where I need to be.

The Crossroads of Destiny

So welcome to the end? Now that you're all caught up, my only question is, "Who is the real protagonist and what is he up to now?" If there's one thing I've learned on this journey, it is that I am not the center of the universe, far from it; and this is far from the end of my story. How can you put an end to a journey that is only now picking up speed? I would like to think that my journey will never be over, but as we all have to cherish our time here on this earth, I will continually strive to expand my perspective and grow as a person, so that I can share my experiences with everyone I meet. Sharing my experiences with others is the skill I hold most dear, because after all, are we all not storytellers at heart? It is one of the most basic human traits. Bonding as a society is what makes us all grow as individuals, and for that, I am grateful.

As I continue to understand my place in this world, I am always reminded of my friends and their place in this story. One of the hardest things to reconcile is losing a friend. No matter how long someone is in your life, once they are gone, there is a gap that is hard to close. I like to say life is all about the people you meet along the way. Cherish every opportunity to make new friends, especially in today's world that is filled with so much turbulence. You can never quantify the impact of being a good friend. I am at peace with the understanding that the paths of others will crisscross the path that I am on, and not everyone is destined to remain in my life. I will forever be in the debt of everyone who I have crossed paths with throughout my life, in the past or future.

They say that no one is ever truly forgotten until no one remembers your name. Who said that? I don't know, really, but I just said it, so it must mean something. People drift out of your life or leave this earth, but that doesn't mean that they are truly gone. The impact they had on your life will stay with you forever, and their love and energy remain with anyone who cares to carry on their stories. I choose to tell their stories. With every story I tell, the energy of that person or people is retained with it.

As I continue to unravel the thread that is my time here on this earth, I can rely on any of the threads I carry around with me for knowledge, experience, love and support. I truly believe that everything happens for a reason, you just have to understand what that reason is. We make our own luck and with the support of my guides and friends who I choose to bring with me wherever I go, I will never truly be alone.

Evan Brown is a nine-year veteran serving in the South Carolina Army National Guard as a Blackhawk Mechanic. He has a professional background in aviation safety and training across multiple different airlines and has developed several standard operating procedures for the safe operations of ground handling personnel at the Charleston (South Carolina) International Airport. Evan has attended the Citadel's undergraduate program for mechanical engineering. Straying from the routine path, he never passes up the opportunity to work in a field unrelated to his schooling. He believes that experiences are more valuable than the stability of an everyday life.

When not working, Evan enjoys spending time hiking, backpacking, and traveling to new destinations in hopes of broadening his perspective. He strives to immerse himself in new cultures and environments so that he may gain more of an insight as to what connects us as humans. He has traveled to many places across Europe, South America, the Middle East, and Asia and has, at every opportunity, tried to immerse himself in the culture of the area.

To see where Evan goes next, follow him on Instagram and Youtube:

@evanbrowndoesstuff

Chapter 3
To Be All I Can Be!
F. Marion Cain, III, LTC, Ret

I thank God for every day I served with the paratroops. When I was assigned to the 82nd Airborne Division at Fort Bragg, North Carolina, after completing Airborne School at Fort Benning, Georgia, it was, if I may paraphrase General Douglas MacArthur, the fulfillment of all my boyish hopes and dreams. I loved serving with the paratroops and was fortunate to spend much of my military career serving with them. Following my time in the 82nd, I was assigned to several posts in the United States, South Korea, Saudi Arabia, and Central and South America, as well as combat deployments in Operation Just Cause (Panama) and Operation Desert Storm (Southwest Asia).

To me, there is no more honorable calling than service in the military. But that service often comes at a price. I was, however, very fortunate. Although I did pay a price for my military service, it was not as high as many others. As I transitioned from my military career into the federal civil service, I began to realize how the many years of pushing myself to my limit, mentally and physically, were taking their toll. It was at this transition point that I started my quest to heal myself.

As I healed myself, however, I quickly realized I was stuck . . . stuck in my past traumas . . . stuck in my old, false beliefs. I began to understand that in order to move to higher levels of awareness and understanding, I first must heal my traumas. As I healed past wounds and traumas, I also began to shed outer layers of heavy energy. As those heavy outer layers shed, I opened to my surroundings, opening and awakening to new and different possibilities I never could have imagined. I began to see people, places, and things differently: to think differently, to become more aware, to become more awake.

When I began my journey of healing and awakening, I assumed my healing would progress in a straight line, at an even pace. In the West we are generally very comfortable with linear thinking, and therefore, we tend to perceive healing as linear, as well. To my surprise, I soon discovered healing is not linear—I experienced my healing journey as a spiral. Once my nervous system became *open* to healing, it began to send me things to heal, starting on the outside of the spiral, with traumas and healing techniques that were already known to me. As I moved further along the spiral, I was exposed to different teachers and techniques, taking me to deeper and deeper levels of healing and awakening.

The first stop on my healing spiral was Tai Chi, followed by yoga and mindfulness. I quickly learned how valuable these practices can be for repairing decades of wounds to the physical, mental, and spiritual body—removing energy blockages in the body and opening the body's energy pathways. As the outer layers of trauma began to shed, I started looking deeper into myself. Remembering Master Yoda's guidance, "You must unlearn what you have learned," I slowed down; instead of looking outward for answers, I focused inward.

Mindfulness can be a powerful practice, because it keeps us in the right relationship with time. There is only now. The future has not yet happened; the past is gone and unchangeable. However, through mindfulness, we can change our relationship with the past, transmuting much of the energetic charge still held in our nervous system —even if the event happened years ago—thus, reshaping our present, as well as our future.

However, I soon learned that the meditative path is not always an easy road to follow. Sometimes, meditation can cause repressed emotions—often traumatic ones—to rise to the surface. Meditation might also trigger uncomfortable or unusual sensations within the body that could be perceived as body pain, headaches, vibrations, or other physical stimuli. Although these symptoms can be startling, they typically are not worrisome. Most people, at some point along their spiritual path, will experience similar occurrences.

Another powerful practice I learned during this period was the use of mantra. Our words have tremendous power, and the chanting of words and mantras has been used for tens of thousands of years to help focus our energy. Mantras are sounds that can be used to change the vibrations of our body, mind, and consciousness, and ultimately, reverberating out into the world at large. This is because sound has enormous power; in fact, it has the power to create an entire universe. Several religious traditions state this quite emphatically. For example, in Christian tradition, God originally manifested as sound: "And God said, "Let there be light. And there was light" (Genesis 1:3), after which, His words created the entire world. According to ancient Indian tradition, in the beginning there was only sound, which reverberated as "Om," and from that sound everything came into existence. In the Bhagavad Gita, Lord Krishna says, "Among rituals, I am the ritual of mantra repetition." The Buddha also extolled the importance and power of sound. Mantra meditation has the power to completely transform our inner energy state transporting, us to higher levels of healing and awakening.

Following yoga, mindfulness, and mantra, I practiced Chod, a Tibetan Buddhist practice that means "cutting through." Chod *cuts through* blockages and obscurations called 'demons'—not external demons, but negative energies held within us. Carl Jung referred to those energies, such as ignorance, anger, fear, and ego, as our Shadow. Chod is performed as a meditative ritual and is often described as walking down a receiving line, shaking hands with your internal demons. Now, meeting your internal demons is not for the faint of heart, but after some time, I was ready to continue along my healing spiral.

As I progressed along my healing journey, I was surprised to discover that trauma can be inherited. Not all our wounds occurred in this lifetime! The energetic imprint of traumatic events can be passed down to us through the generations. Additionally, the energetic imprint of wounds received in past lives can be passed down to us, as we reincarnate through space and time. It took a while for me to get into the whole past life thing. But as I dove deeper into my meditation practice, I began to experience memories and sensations that I knew were not from my current life.

My next big shift occurred while I worked in the Pentagon. Every few months, a group of Wounded Warriors from Walter Reed National Military Medical Center, along with their family members, would tour the Pentagon. During these visits, Pentagon employees—almost all of whom are active-duty service members, veterans, or family members—stood in the hallways and greeted them with applause. As I watched this procession, I saw, firsthand, the costs of war on our youngest and newest veterans. I resolved to do what I could to assist those heroes and their families.

After discussing my concerns with my wife, we consulted with our yoga teacher. Through our discussions, we learned that by working somatically, we could heal the trauma held in the nervous system, specifically in the vagus nerve. Certain alternative health modalities are particularly effective at working with trauma in the central nervous system, such as Somatic Experiencing® (SE) and Biodynamic Craniosacral Therapy (BCST); with training, we could use these modalities to help not only ourselves but others, as well.

By studying SE®, my wife and I began to understand trauma at a much deeper level—almost all trauma manifests as an uncompleted fight, flight, or freeze response stuck in the body. SE® helps us release that stuck energy, recover, and become more resilient. We next dove into BCST, a healing art that supports nervous system regulation and mitigates the effects of stress and trauma. BCST sessions are very relaxing for the mind and body; health is experienced as more accessible and embodied.

Following our SE® and BCST training, we decided to study Reiki, an energy healing system which originated in Japan. Reiki works by raising our vibration and stimulating the body's innate healing system. A Reiki session assists the body in returning to balance, creating an improved state of health and well-being. Many of our ailments are caused by mental and emotional imbalances in our bodies—SE®, BCST, and Reiki are very effective tools to bring those imbalances to the surface and remove them, reducing stress and anxiety, and encouraging relaxation.

Next, I was led to study the Akashic Records, an energetic "recording" of every thought, word, deed, motive, intention, and feeling a soul has ever experienced since its first incarnation into a physical form. Your Record is like an in-depth autobiography, written without judgment regarding choices made or outcomes manifested. It interacts with the soul's present experience, because all past experiences and thoughts influence what is being attracted into one's life now. Past experiences also affect how one responds, relates, or reacts to their life in the present moment. I found the Akashic Records to be an excellent source of guidance, especially regarding healing wounds from my past lives and uncovering any unconscious beliefs that were holding me back.

Following careers in the United States Army and Federal Civil Service, I returned to my boyhood home on the farm, where I was able to reestablish my connection with nature. Naturally, earth medicine seemed like the next logical step on my journey of healing and awakening. I had always been interested in Shamanism, perhaps the earth's oldest religion, but I was never able to find a suitable teacher. Finally, after retiring from military and government service, I discovered a fellow Army veteran and seventh-generation Native American medicine woman, who uses a traditional Native American medicine wheel for two very effective healing processes. One focused on healing the chakras; she calls the practice "deep animal healing." The other process is called "the fractured horse," used to repair and heal relationships.

I found earth medicine to be not only practicable but also very valuable. Of all the healing modalities I have studied and practiced, earth medicine is, by far, one of the most effective, the most healing. It has taken me a lifetime to reach this level, and earth medicine seems to be the final stop on my healing spiral. There is so much more to learn, though; I imagine I will need the rest of my life to delve deeper into this fascinating healing modality.

As I traveled along my healing spiral, I learned many important lessons about myself and about healing, in general. As my wife and I deepened our study of trauma, we were saddened to realize that standard treatments for Post-traumatic Stress Disorder (PTSD) consist mostly of medications and traditional talk therapy. It is my perspective that medications, generally, do not resolve trauma; they simply suppress the symptoms. Talk therapies can help up to a point, but talking keeps us in our neocortex, the portion of our brain responsible for most higher-order functions, such as critical thinking, problem-solving, decision-making, and spirituality. Talking about our traumas will not reach into the body's autonomic nervous system or affect the "reptilian brain," therefore, talking about our ordeal will not resolve trauma held in the central nervous system.

I also realized, very early in my journey, we must do the "inner work," which typically means addressing the shadow side. As I healed, I found myself becoming less judgmental. I was able to develop understanding and compassion for myself, as well as others. I was able to love myself.

Another of my most important lessons was understanding that *it's all about energy*. Albert Einstein made several notable statements related to energy. Two of my favorites are:

> *"Everything is energy, and that's all there is to it. Match the frequency of the reality you want, and you cannot help but get that reality. It can be no other way. This is not philosophy; this is physics."*

> *"Energy cannot be created or destroyed, it can only be changed from one form to another."*

In other words, energy can be transmuted. Once we accept that everything is energy, vibrating at different frequencies, and that this energy can be transformed into a different state, an entire world of healing opens to us! We begin to understand that by changing our energy state, we change our internal state, which in turn, changes the world around us.

Our energy field, together with our diet and lifestyle, greatly influence our health and emotions. When we leave toxic energies unchecked, we succumb to a fate infused with disease and suffering, instead of discovering our divine destiny. As we begin to balance our internal energy, we reach a state in which synchronicity just happens, with seemingly little effort on our part.

I also learned how important it is to break free of "time." We tend to think of time as linear, like a river flowing steadily in a single direction. But what if time is nonlinear, more like a lake, on which we can move in different directions? Consider . . . the future exists, but it has not yet happened; therefore, it exists only in *potential possibilities*. The future is not fixed; rather, it is determined by the energy of our actions and thoughts *today*. As we shift our energy, the potentials of our future also shift to match our changed energy state. Similarly, the past has already happened, but we can transmute the energies associated with the past that we harbor within our memory and body.

Along the way, I also learned that crystals, because they vibrate at such a high frequency, can help us transmute our energies and assist us in harmonizing and balancing the frequency of our energy field. Many people believe the specific frequencies and colors of quartz crystals are related to emotional, spiritual, and physical issues and can be used for healing. Quartz crystals have long fascinated scientists and spiritualists alike; Nikola Tesla was no exception, stating, "If you want to find the secrets of the universe, think in terms of energy, frequency, and vibration." His experiments with quartz crystals led him to believe in their potential to revolutionize energy production.

Lastly, as I immersed myself in the study of trauma healing modalities, I came to understand that trauma can be layered. For example, if a wound is experienced in early childhood, over time, other wounds layer upon it, such that the initial injury is no longer in our awareness . . . it's been forgotten.

An additional benefit to healing and transmuting your energy is that the people and things you don't need in your life begin to fall away. You start to pay attention to your needs, your boundaries.

I thank God for the wonderful teachers I met along my journey. Wisdom traditions tell us, "The teacher appears when the student is ready." This means we need to reach a certain level of maturity, understanding, or openness to be able to embrace new guidance and wisdom. We discover the wisdom that stems from inner stillness and silence and become aware of the ebbs and flows of life itself. Throughout my journey of healing and awakening, I've been very fortunate to have many wonderful teachers and mentors, each one taking me deeper and deeper into my journey of healing and awakening. I owe them my deepest gratitude. But perhaps my greatest teacher has been my wife, who has been with me every step of the way.

"Trauma is not a life sentence."
— Dr. Peter Levine

Marion Cain served twenty-six years with the United States Army, serving as a Master Parachutist. His assignments include the 82nd Airborne Division and the United States Army Special Operations Command, as well as Saudi Arabia, South Korea, and Panama. Marion is a veteran of operational deployments for Operations Just Cause (Panama) and Desert Storm (Southwest Asia).

A Registered Professional Engineer, Certified Associate Program Manager, Somatic Experiencing Practitioner, and Registered Craniosacral Therapist, Marion's civilian education includes a Bachelor of Science in Civil Engineering from The Citadel, a Master of Science in Civil Engineering from the University of California at Berkeley, and a Master of Military Art and Science from the United States Army School of Advanced Military Studies. His military education also includes the Defense Language Institute and the Inter-American Defense College.

While stationed in Panama, Marion coordinated road construction in the Ecuadorian rainforest and later commanded a battalion task force to the Andes Mountains to enlarge the runway at Potosi, Bolivia. This marked the first large-scale, high-altitude deployment of the United States Army to altitudes of more than eleven-thousand feet since World War II. While assigned to the Pentagon, he led the planning and coordination of Department of Defense security and logistics support to the 1996 Atlanta Olympics and 1997 Presidential Inaugural.

Following retirement from military service, Marion served as Deputy Director and then Director of the Center for Domestic Preparedness, in Anniston, Alabama. The center provides advanced, hands-on training in responding to terrorist attacks using weapons of mass destruction. Under his leadership, the center grew from training 1,800 emergency responders a year, to becoming the second largest training center in the Department of Homeland Security, employing a staff of over 960 and training more than 61,500 emergency responders a year.

Later, while assigned to the Office of the Secretary of Defense Marion's responsibilities included the streamlining of the civilian credentialing process for service members and veterans. Marion worked with the National Economic Council and the Executive Office of the First Lady to eliminate barriers to credentialing for service members and veterans. He was also responsible for establishing the Skill Bridge program to assist service members in their transition to civilian employment. Marion served as a co-lead for the Education and Training Work Group of the President's Department of Defense/Veterans Affairs Veterans Employment Task Force.

Since retiring from government service, Marion and his wife, Parham, established a practice in Sumter, South Carolina focused on restoring health to veterans, accident victims, and victims of abuse, through alternative and holistic health methodologies.

Learn more about Marion at www.nextmissiontherapy.com.

Chapter 4
Is It Over Yet?
Samantha Love Kaufman

The pain of betrayal is agonizing. I lie here, curled into a fetal position in a plush, high-backed, hotel room chair, as the air conditioning blows warm air loudly onto my already tear-induced, feverish body. I am in my son's college town, meant to be meeting him shortly, as he reached out to me in a near catatonic state of confusion over what he wants to do with his life.

And here I sit, a total wreck in my hotel room, asking myself over and over: What did I do? What did I say to get banished? Why would they, my "spiritual" friends, be so cruel as to suddenly lock me out of our metaphysical Facebook group, unfriend me and turn their backs on me?

What words of advice can I possibly offer him when I am in absolute, utter despair, wracked by sobs, anxiety, a never-ending parade of questions like vultures circling my mind as if I am emotional carrion. And if I can't rationally resolve these questions, they will descend and peck at my fragile sense of spiritual identity until I am nothing.

I am nothing. I am nothing to these people who claimed me as one of their own, who asked me to step up into the light, bask at the adoration of others and lead alongside them. I thought I had arrived. I thought I had been given the green light by my spirit guides and this was it—the beginning of my metaphysical legacy.

Not. Even. Close.

This was just yet another step in the unfoldment of my awakening journey. We often cannot see when we are on the journey to awakening. It can only be seen, in hindsight, once we have had the time to process yet another excruciatingly painful lesson. Must they always be painful?

I suppose they must. It seems we must keep tearing down the ego, flail it into submission, then nearly obliterate it to become the next best version of whoever we are meant to be—much like the phoenix rising from the ashes. And along the way, we pick ourselves up, dust ourselves off and realize we have earned a new badge, a new level of awareness and an all-new perception of what it is we are becoming. What is it I am becoming?

In 1989, I married a narcissist. Like a hairy, wolfish spider, he carefully crafted a web of false beliefs around me, causing me to doubt myself, my self-worth. Then I realized, too late, the trap had already sprung and I found myself completely alienated from family and friends. I should've known better.

The series of incidents that led me to that painful era of my life was the moment my unfoldment began in earnest. My dating and subsequent marriage to this monster was as inevitable as the very breath I took for granted. It was as if I was caught up in the flow of events beyond my control, like being caught in a riptide where there is nothing left to do but let go. At the time, I didn't recognize it as such. It's only by looking back that I can clearly recognize those pivotal moments of growth. Those divinely orchestrated moments filled with spiritual wonder and awe. And there were so many - too many for this accounting.

When you can't express outwardly, I think you begin to express inwardly. That way lies madness, I know. I think you begin to go so deeply within that you are no longer actually bound by the "within," but you discover a doorway to a whole other universe. I think I was well on my way to that discovery, in time, but this period of my life was the catalyst.

I sought out therapy for support. My therapist was an elderly ex-cowboy with a penchant for curse words and unconventional therapy. The evolution of my therapy occurred in three stages. Stage One: Sam wonders how she can be such a broken individual and works earnestly to find the broken pieces to fix herself. Stage Two: Sam realizes she has been duped by a master manipulator, a narcissist, and begins exploring early childhood and past life regression to heal from and prevent these wounds from repeating themselves. Stage Three: Sam learns that it is okay to have boundaries, to have a sense of Self and to be loved, and begins to understand the mechanisms to begin disentangling herself from her prison of a marriage.

I drew, from deep within, the strength of a myriad other Me's who had been persecuted throughout lifetimes. I was unrecognizable to myself as I lost my mind and gave myself over to some other greater force, a greater Me. I left without realizing I was leaving. I left my cat. I left all my belongings. And with my two-year-old daughter's hand in mine, I left.

Thus, my spiritual journey began to take shape. I met my first mentor who introduced me to Tarot. She taught me that there truly are angels among us, as she took a veritable stranger into her home, while I fought for primary custody of my daughter and sorted through the detritus of the illusion of a marriage. Ultimately, I won freedom for both myself and my daughter.

My spiritual education expanded over the coming years through unusual mechanisms. I would walk into a bookstore, head over to the spiritual/metaphysical section and invariably find one book set out amongst the others. It didn't matter if it was out of order within a series. It would always contain the next bit of information I needed to know for the next practical application in my life. It's like my guides were saying, "Here, this is what you now need to understand."

Around 1998, I discovered medium Sylvia Brown and her unabashedly raw way of expressing the spiritual world. I felt like I had found a true compatriot. I realized the rules for spiritual communication were too confining, that I was a "rules-breaker," and I felt she gave me permission to simply be me and follow my heart and passion. During this time, I began studying past life regression and automatic-writing.

In 1999, I remarried, and in 2000, my son came into the world. During my pregnancy, I would hold my belly and whisper his name as Daniel, even though I knew we were going to call him by another name. Still, I could not let go of Daniel. I felt prompted to do an auto-matic-writing session to uncover who Daniel was to me. Through the process, I came to understand that he had been my little brother in a past life, a life that I was able to date and place on a map. I asked why I was his mother in this lifetime. It was explained to me that I had taken too much responsibility for him in the last lifetime, so I was given this lifetime in an even closer role, yet I was meant to step back and allow him to become his own person. So from day one, I guided him along his journey with that thought as my guiding light.

Looking back, this and following events were a way of winnowing me from the "muggle" herd. (I borrowed the term *muggle* from the Harry Potter series, defined as those who are unaware of the unseen world.) They shifted my perspective in such a way as to have me operating in a totally "outside the box" reality that left me with no discernable frame of reference. There was a lot of "figuring it out" as I went. It was as if I was leapfrogging from one temporary platform of understanding and reality to the next.

I recall a massive perspective shift that occurred while visiting my in-laws in Ohio in the Spring of 2002. I was reading one of the *Conversations with God* books by Neale Donald Walsch. It was late at night, my husband was asleep, and I recognized that within whatever it was I was reading, a huge epiphany was forming. I must have read until 3 a.m. I recall waking up the next morning, looking out the window, and realizing everything had changed. It was like perceiving a whole new level of awareness . . . as if reality was stacked upon itself. I felt I was observing everything through a glass wall. I could interact with others, but I could sense and perceive so much more than them; however, I didn't really understand what I was perceiving. Reality had literally shifted for me. It only lasted for so long—days, maybe weeks, or perhaps I just got used to the perceptual awareness. I'm not sure, but life stepped in, and I moved on.

There were times when I would get lost in "muggle" world, but not for long. These periods of time were rest periods. Periods for me to integrate what I had learned and to experience other life lessons that would help me to grow in empathy and understanding. And then, BAM—a day would happen upon me that would alter my current path and send me down a metaphysical rabbit hole.

These would be fascinating encounters with unusual individuals or seemingly lofty spiritual teachers. I would learn new perspectives on spiritual thought or metaphysical practices such as offering *light* to purify the body and food. Concepts about energy, vibration, and the frequency of healing. And always, throughout, somehow people would find me, and I would offer my tarot readings to them.

My Tarot readings began to take on a nuance of emotional healing. As a psychic, (I prefer the word *intuitive*), I was always drawn to reveal that dark shadow, deep within someone, that needed to come to light. I would bring about this awareness and shift their perception about people and circumstances. I often say about my readings, "It always ends in tears." They are definitely not for "entertainment purposes only."

I recall passing days, sharing ideas with an office mate of how we could draw nourishment and energy from the trees around us. This was in my *The Celestine Prophecy* (by James Redfield) phase. It was like I couldn't get enough. Metaphysical concepts were the very air I would breathe. I would hunger for them. And then, like a shade being drawn, it would vanish, and I would emerge back into "muggle" world . . . bleary-eyed, lost, and confused. That is also when crises of one sort or another would crop up in my life, and I would go through profound mental and physical hardships, designed to cause me to question existence, pain, people, motives, cause, and effect.

In 2003, I was desperately seeking community, as I was so tired of being on this solitary spiritual journey. I discovered my community in much the same way as Goldilocks found her happy place. I happened upon the Unitarian Church—lovely people, but they were too intellectual for what I was seeking at the time. And just like the story of *Goldilocks and the Three Bears*, I look back on this and think, *this bed was too hard*. Then I happened upon the Unity Church. However, the Unity members were overflowing with love and acceptance to the point of overwhelming my then personal boundaries. *This bed seemed way too soft*. So I backed off and resumed my solitary spiritual journey.

I came across the works of Marianne Williamson's, *A Course in Miracles,* and felt kinship once again. This led me to a group study being offered by the same Unity Church members. Over a year had passed since I had last darkened that doorway. With some reluctance and a burning desire to immerse myself in spiritual studies, I felt compelled to attend a session. They had changed. Or, rather, I had changed. I felt open and receptive. I basked in their warmth and cheer. And while *A Course in Miracles* was not for me, the Unity Church now was. *This bed was just right.*

Within Unity, I found a new friend, and we laughed, played, and explored together. She became my next mentor; she taught me how to leave the Tarot cards behind and trust in the messages my guides were sending me. I also came across the work of Abraham-Hicks, and my spiritual unfoldment was accelerated. In 2005, I began publishing my own spiritual magazine and directory, *Mind, Body & Soul*. I put on metaphysical fairs and film screenings. Looking back, maybe this was indicative of the first tremors of my full-on awakening experience.

Then one day, it just happened. I can't recall exactly how it happened, but I suddenly was thrust into a dual existence. I had been playing around with automatic-writing and past life regression. I was raising a five-year-old boy; my thirteen-year-old daughter was going through something I could not quite put my finger on at the time, but it was not good. I was creating websites for a living and would have an occasional reading client. Life was busy and overwhelming.

I recall doing a past life regression, but instead of going somewhere in the past, I suddenly saw me, or the essence of me, in a time out of time. I was in a paddock, of sorts, on the ground in the dirt, but the dirt wasn't really dirt. It was the concept of dirt—as if there was nothing around me until I thought about my surroundings. Then, I could see a barn, and I could make out a fence. I asked myself what I was doing here. I was flooded with a sudden knowingness.

I knew who I was on the other side. I referred to myself as Tantra. I understood that my current interest was in understanding how to make the life forms of animals more compatible, harmonious, and happier on Earth. It is a far more complex task than one might imagine. At the time I was realizing all of this, I didn't have the vocabulary, the understanding that I now possess. I can now say I knew these were thought forms that I was playing with, that I was creating patterns based on frequency that would exist and behave in a specific way once on Earth. I was adapting them to environments and to benefit the humans.

It was as if an eternal flame sprung to light within me. An unshakeable knowingness. I knew who I was! At least, I knew of an aspect of who I was. Maybe it is better to say, I was at the very start of an understanding that I was/am more than what I thought I was/am. At some point, the word *duality* popped into my head. And this was before I had ever heard the expression.

I knew I was a soul and that I had lived many lives. What my awareness was now integrating was that I wasn't only existing in this physical time-space reality, but I existed outside of it, as well, simultaneously. This epiphany reminded me of that earlier awareness of the overlay of reality I had experienced back in Ohio.

Driving my car around on errands and seeing all the colors around me infused with a greater vibrance, it was like they were vibrating and calling to me. I felt such a wave of homesickness wash over me. At first, I felt that this 3-D reality was a lie, a façade. And yet, what kept me tied to this space and time were my two children. It's not that I felt suicidal, I just wanted to go *home*. It called to me. It vibrated through my very being.

This duality lasted for roughly two weeks. Honestly, I probably should not have been driving my car during this phase, as reality was not hard and fast. It was malleable. It was left open to interpretation. I cannot recollect how I pulled back, but I recall feeling that my children needed their mother, and I had to make a conscious choice. I chose them.

Was this it? Was this my great awakening? Yes and no. I think it has been unfolding over time. It most likely started when I was a child, and I believe it is still unfolding even now. To awaken means to become aware of something. On this journey, I am forever becoming aware of a greater understanding, a greater mystery. Honestly, you never "arrive."

After integrating the agonizing experience I described at the beginning of this chapter, I have become aware that my solitary journey has been purposeful; that each time I found community and had it subsequently stripped from me, it was so that I would not get indoctrinated with a single idea, methodology, or dogmatism. This has led me on a path to greater independent growth. While it has been incredibly painful to go from camaraderie to betrayal, it has helped me to understand the importance of "walking our talk" and treating people by the Golden Rule. It is the path I continue to take every day.

As my awareness grows, my vocabulary grows, my abilities grow, and my compassion and love for humanity grows. I am able to hold many simultaneous truths from a variety of perspectives and honor each one. My mind continues to expand so that it can integrate many levels of understanding, so that it isn't a "this *or* that," but a "this *and* that." While I do not have *blind* trust—as this is a realm for the physical, the nature of contrast—I have learned to exercise my discernment and spend most of my days in a positive, high-vibe space, with the awareness that this experience is truly benevolent and loving.

Remember . . .

You are loved beyond your ability to comprehend!

Samantha Love Kaufman offers her skills and savvy in the Intuitive Arts of Tarot, psychic readings, mediumship, and spiritual life coaching. She is often quoted as saying she is a "jack-of-all-trades and master-of-none," meaning she acknowledges that one never fully *arrives*. Samantha's experiences keep moving her in an ever-widening arc of experiential learning designed to integrate a wide range or modalities into her spiritual and metaphysical practice.

Joining her in this manic adventure are her husband and her two adult children, as well as her soul kitty, Pantalimon, two older cats, a revolving door of foster kitties, and some truly fabulous friends. They are all a wonderful source of love, companionship, and support, from which she draws a great deal of experience, offering her the opportunity to practice, daily, the art of *walking her talk* and refining her spiritual awareness.

Additionally, Samantha co-hosts two podcasts. *Out On A Limb* is a spiritual/metaphysical podcast in which she and her two co-hosts interview fellow practitioners and explore a variety of fascinating topics. *KISS – Keep It Simple, Sister* is a spiritual life coaching podcast that Samantha co-hosts with Diana Sullivan, that includes a women's only Facebook group component to further individual growth and camaraderie through community.

A Fire Within Me is the name of Samantha's practice and website. Being that she is a triple fire, Aries, it just made sense. There are many resources to be found on the website including wellness guides and the opportunity for a free "WTH Happened to My Life?" audit and follow-up Zoom session. Notices for upcoming courses and masterclasses ranging from Tarot to Life Design will be found there, as well.

Samantha can be reached via her website: www.AFireWithin.Me

Chapter 5
Chrysanthemum Tea
Jim Roach, MD

Pleasant, elderly Anne, a gentle presence with Native American heritage, rocked my world.

After thirty years of medical practice, my mind was searching. Broad new possibilities were opening. Stories filtered in. I wanted so much to learn more. Transcendent quantum physics, metaphysical accounts shared by a mentor, energy healing, spiritual near-death experiences (NDEs)—I was beginning to understand. New patients were prodded when they came as to any mystical experiences they could share. While sometimes revealing they had never told anyone, not even their spouse, they fortunately trusted I could keep and validate their secrets.

Growing up, Anne was neglected by her mother. Claire, a kind neighborly woman, took Anne under her wing, serving as mother and mentor. Decades later Anne suddenly awoke in the middle of the night, shaken by a vivid dream: Claire was riding through her front yard on a "choo choo" train, leaning out, shouting, "Toot, toot!" Anne glanced at the clock: 1:20 a.m.

As she came downstairs that morning, the phone rang. She answered, knowingly.

"What time did she die?"

"2:20 a.m."—but a time zone away.

At Claire's visitation, Anne gushed her dream to the greeter. Astonished, the greeter held up four fingers: "You are the fourth person with the identical story!" The others, too, had been close to Claire, shepherded and supported as Anne had been.

* * *

My curiosity began as a teenager, after finding a book on Edgar Cayce, the "sleeping prophet" and "father of holistic medicine." His incredible story opened my understanding of spirituality and raised the possibility of reincarnation. On reflection, it also explains my becoming the first integrative holistic medicine physician in Kentucky. A Harvard theology student told me that understanding trauma in a previous lifetime gave him profound healing in this one. The University of Virginia School of Medicine Division of Perceptual Studies has studied this extensively for *sixty* years; after 2,300 cases, have they essentially proven reincarnation?

After joining family medicine with my father, I became restless for greater pursuits. This led to Habitat for Humanity, tackling tobacco addiction, and learning communication and philosophies promoted by Wayne Dyer and Deepak Chopra. Turning fifty, striving for optimal longevity and wellness, I sought national nutritional, botanical, and holistic conferences not allied with drug companies; I am now witness to fifty of those, linked with the country's top integrative holistic healers. Add twenty thousand hours of study and my horizon expanded immensely.

In 2004, after two of Andrew Weil, MD's Nutrition and Health conferences, Weil offered a botanical conference at Columbia University in New York City, at the time an unattractive venue; after visits in my youth, I had no desire to return. I would never use botanicals in my practice . . . or so I thought.

But a potent, intuitive yearning captured my heart. Edgar Cayce's seed of holistic curiosity aroused my soul. Was this pre-destiny? It was a massively pivotal point in my life. I learned of the botanical Rhodiola rosea. The Soviet's gave Rhodiola to Olympic athletes to improve performance; given to college students the week before and during exams, they scored one grade better. What a powerhouse! Herbs *were* truly more than a placebo. Rhodiola rosea energized me and boosted my spirits and productivity, while thickening my skin. This exploration snow-balled into trips to Ashland, Oregon to study under the guru of botanical medicine, Donnie Yance. Becoming the top botanical physician in the country, soon I achieved patient outcomes I had not known possible, the best of any Kentucky physician over ensuing years. Cancer was the ultimate menace to conquer; Donnie's guidance led to a national cancer clientele and authoring one of the best, integrative cancer books in the United States. What an incredibly intuitive moment that had been!

At a holistic conference outside Austin, I met its head, Robert Anderson, MD. On a long, wooded walk, Bob shared of a night he was aroused by a bright, glowing ball outside his bedroom window. An omen? He searched the house. Finding a smoking iron ready to catch flame, he rushed it out. Back in his bedroom, the glowing ball had left. No neighbors witnessed this. He knew it was divine. Dr. Anderson's candid reflection of this astounding event mesmerized me.

Five years later, an old church acquaintance, after wrecking her car, described floating above, looking down. It was so blissful she became irate after falling back into her body. Her focus now was to help others. She no longer feared death. What if I did not fear death?

What if I could convince my patients not to fear death? *What a preposterous thought!* I recall reflecting. Yet, now, that is exactly what I do.

In stark contrast, an alcoholic revealed a frightening, spiritual near-death experience (NDE) with details he would not share. He stopped drinking immediately and did all he could to make amends. Years later in an ICU, he again witnessed the beyond, this time blissfully.

Koleoso's experience was more profound. With the Vietnam War raging, he knew to join the Armed Forces rather than be drafted, so he could choose his base—Okinawa, Japan. Young, restless, and reckless, speedily careening in his jeep, Koleoso missed a cliff, veering headlong into a building, launching an NDE. Immense, infinite love enveloped him with a knowing of the divinity. After the war, Koleoso relentlessly traveled the world searching for his spiritual path. But ten years later, Koleoso began to doubt. "God, prove to me the reality of you."

A car crossed four lanes of traffic and T-boned his, crumpled his face and ripped his nose halfway off. In a new NDE, he sat on a chair, naked, in the middle of New York City, unable to escape. It turned dark. Koleoso, now floating down a river, saw Beings standing on the bank, whom he intuited were ancestors. Light emerged, and he felt the powerful presence of Jesus. The living consciousness of everything around him, even pebbles, he recognized. All was love.

Koleoso and his gifted wife, Ossunike, invited me one evening, in a special ritual, to consult the Oracles. Their answer as to my name raised Ossunike's eyebrows—*Imhotep* . . . the first physician, noted astronomer, and architect, in 3000 BC Egypt. To this day, I continue my search to fully grasp the name's importance, especially since later being told I had a previous Egyptian life.

As patients' spiritual stories poured forth, I noticed commonalities. Women and men with estrogen-related health concerns were sensitive, wired, intuitive, and divinely connected—owners of what I called "the God gene."

As I began to grasp quantum physics and energy healing, a right shoulder rotator cuff tear tested this reality. At a holistic conference, I asked a panel for recommendations, to no avail. Afterwards, an Asian Reiki Master approached—would I like to be healed? "Yes!" Putting his hands above my shoulders, he asked what came to mind. My eyes teared as I recalled being unable to say goodbye to my mother when she died after a car accident, New Year's Eve, 1994. On arising the next morning, my shoulder was well!

As my wife and I walked through my small town, evenings after work, streetlights, at times, would blink on or off. They mainly went off—in fact, seven of eight times. They turned *off* on days of good deeds but *on* when I could have done better.

In a dream one night, I sat alone in my church pew, my church empty. A bubble descended from the ceiling, soon filling my full visual field and accompanied by a surprising physical warmth. Inside the bubble, the gentle face of Grandmother Roach offered a soft, kind smile. After lingering, the bubble slowly rose to the ceiling, and as it left, so did the warmth. Never before or since have I felt a physical warmth in a dream.

I dreamt of a factory floor at a forty-five-degree view, with nearly one thousand people in one-piece, bright yellow outfits. It was so vivid that I told my wife and e-mailed my daughter. A week later, a picture was taken at the Austin Gigafactory of the first Cybertruck coming off the assembly line. My top stock holding was Tesla. A week later, in an online shareholder report, the identical image of my dream appeared . . . in a picture taken at a 45-degree angle, nearly a thousand factory workers with bright, yellow vests surrounded the first Cybertruck on the large factory floor.

My wife, Dee, was receptionist when Mariam, a new patient seen a month earlier, appeared at the front desk asking to be seen. Dee explained that my appointments were booked months out, but sensing Mariam's urgency, Dee knew to work her in. When I walked into the patient room, Mariam immediately said, "You are probably going to think I am crazy but . . . . "

Mariam had three NDEs, which made her especially intuitive. Living with her husband in Colorado, a haunting riddle came to mind—the word "Ashland" and the image of a college on a hill. She didn't know its meaning but knew she had to solve it. This riddle compelled her to, futilely, travel to Ashland, Oregon. Then after moving to central Kentucky, Mariam visited me at my office. Outside my small town was a college on a hill; I was a trustee. A YouTube search revealed my testimonial for Mederi Foundation . . . in Ashland, Oregon. *I was the connection.*

Mariam gently grasped successive fingertips as if they carried secret meaning. "The conference you are planning at Midway College next month is supposed to happen. That's the message I am to convey. It is a powerful message, because it caused me to visit Ashland, Oregon, my family to move to Kentucky, and for me to see you to deliver this message." I had told no one that I had planned to host my conference at Midway College. But Mariam somehow knew. Indeed, just the month before, I decided to have a conference, but due to the high price, just a few had signed up. I was being told not to cancel. The message landed powerfully! A decade later, my successful conferences continue, imparting holistic knowledge and spirituality.

In planning a trip to the National Publicity Summit (NPS) in New York City, I asked Koleoso if the trip was worth it. His tarot cards said yes. The summit led to participation with Steve Harrison's Quantum Leap program in Philadelphia, where I met many other aspiring authors and later connected with Jack Canfield. Extraordinarily, *most* participants had experienced transformative spiritual events, from NDEs, to astral-travel, to reincarnation.

While completing *God's House Calls*, I prayed for more exceptional stories to bolster its impact. Flying from the Philadelphia meeting to present at Mayo Clinic, the connection in Chicago would be tight. I prayed that I was open to God's direction; if I didn't make the connection, I accepted it had purpose. Just missing it, I got the last seat on the next plane for Minnesota—next to one of the most intuitive individuals I had ever met. At the hotel, the two midnight receptionists shared unimaginably provocative stories. Together these led to a riveting chapter in my book.

To magnify the stark dangers of Rx medicine and the remarkable, at times miraculous, healing capacity of nutrients and botanicals, I wrote *Brilliance*. It unveiled my bewildering quantum metaphysical world, with UFO and extra-terrestrial (ET) stories, including a Catholic priest experiencing a UFO with a translation device, and a theologian's NDE involving three ETs. Thirty-five have now shared UFO stories, including a college religion professor witnessing a 300-foot UFO at tree-top level and a retired lawyer, who saw UFOs twice, once up close. Fifteen have had face-to-face ET encounters, one noting it was completely foreign to any comic depictions.

For further insights, at meditation and fasting retreats I sank into a trance, words rising from my subconscious. My Higher Self reminded me of a traumatic spanking with details I had not recalled. Jumping from the edge of a dark cliff, I soared, viewing my body below. I sensed the incredible presence of the divine, my true home. Valuable health messages came through, helping both me and my patients. It was unbelievably revealing, giving my book a new, surreal perspective. A series of these experiences led to a profound, exhilarating awakening.

After attending my first botanical retreat, where I offered great praise to Jesus and God, I walked through my hometown, Midway. Inexplicably, I went upstairs to a hidden art shop which I rarely visit. Just inside the door, I spied a drawing of Jesus, not yet signed, by artist Debbie Graviss. I had to have it! Displayed at the end of my downstairs hall, the portrait is a little like the Mona Lisa: Is he smiling or is he not? He nearly always has a gentle smile but sometimes not, so I pay attention.

As a tiny tot, Don Coffey had a phenomenal, transformative spiritual experience, unlike any I had heard. Later, after attending his spiritual NDE group, he suggested I might be interested in L/L Research.[1] Yes!

In Mayfield, Kentucky, in 1949, there were thirty sightings of UFOs. The call went out to Ft. Knox to investigate. Three pilots were sent up. One, indeed, identified a large metallic UFO. Following it to twenty thousand feet, he lost oxygen, crashed, and died. Don Ellis, a nineteen-year-old understudy, saddened and intrigued, traveled the country for the next twenty-five years, investigating UFO incidents. Then, as professor of physics at the University of Louisville, a student associate of his, Carla Rueckert, when in a deep meditative state, began channeling a voice from the Universe. From 1981 to 1984, she channeled Ra, a self-described sixth-density, social memory complex, leading to two, thick books, including fascinating world history on Egypt and Atlantis, cushioned with universal wisdom. This melded into Q'uo, who has communicated regularly for forty-three years to a small group in Louisville who, together, have written ten books, translated into as many as twenty-four languages.

Q'uo is of service to one loving, powerful Creator, to which we are all a part. At L/L meetings, channeled answers offer advice and insights but cannot interfere with free will, due to universal agreement about

---

1. Home of The Law of One material, L/L Research is a non-profit organization dedicated to discovering and sharing information to aid in the spiritual evolution of humankind (https://www.llresearch.org/).

Earth. Over two years, Q'uo has answered my questions, imparting profound wisdom and tear-promoting compassion.

"What is the root psychological cause of cancer?"

"Anger" was the reply.

"What is the impact of multiple people praying or intending together for the same outcome?"

"Each added person doubles the impact."

At the International Association of Near-Death Studies (IANDS) 2022 conference, I presented on "The God Gene" and heard Dr. Jeffrey Mishlove's award-winning presentation on proof of an after-life. As the world's only PhD in parapsychology, he has done capti-vating interviews for forty years on metaphysical topics. These weekly interviews on newthinkingallowed.org have vastly stretched my universe. Ten thousand schools teaching ESP in China? A man who could trigger thunderstorms and UFO appearances? A psychic surgeon who healed hundreds of thousands? How special to be inter-viewed on his show about my patients' mystical experiences!

At lunch at the next IANDS conference, Jeffrey announced a desire for an initiative to end mass gun violence. Did he want me to ask Q'uo that question? Jeffrey: "Tell them to end this mess." Q'uo's response was for a large number to meditate on surrounding those contemplating violence with a cylinder of light that forced them to reflect before acting.

With a strong desire to spread the quantum physics message, I asked my minister if I could give a sermon. The response: Consider a Sunday school class. In my small church, that would mean only a handful of attendees. But contemplating, what if I took out a full-page, color advertisement—in the *Lexington Herald-Leader* which reaches tens of thousands—promoting the class with a free breakfast? What if I mentioned conversations with ETs in the ad? Instead of three showing up, eighty came! Like an old-fashioned revival, it attracted intuitives who knew there is more to this existence and were hungry to learn. It was a resounding success.

One full table at these Sunday sessions was occupied by fans of Samuel. Lea Shultz has been a trance channel for Samuel for a remarkable forty years. Samuel speaks in a Scottish brogue, with a sharp wit, imparting great wisdom of the ages, personal advice, and preparation for the coming chaotic but ultimately triumphant ascendance into fifth density.

A gifted friend suggested I check in with a trance channeler in pursuing my metaphysical journey. Connecting with my Higher Self in this way provided tremendous insight, perspective, and guidance. While a healer in this life, in every other past lifetime my Higher Self said I have been a shaman, oracle, and healer. Does that explain my Imhotep name? From my ancient personal heritage, healing will continue into future non-physical dimensions.

Each morning, I sip chrysanthemum tea on my back porch, looking out on my yard. Feeders brim with sunflower seed, attracting cardinals, goldfinch, and squirrels. I could have retired three years ago, but enjoying my unique calling, I now plan to work as long as I am able.

If my patients' NDEs have taught me anything, it is that God is love. While the alcoholic had a terrifying NDE—attempted suicides trigger horrific NDEs as wake up calls, and visits to Hell-like settings presage the angst of desolate separation from God—by far, most NDErs of all religions and even atheists bask in the ultimate bliss of our Creator's love. NDErs always come back LESS religious, LESS dogmatic, but MORE loving. Our Maker is responsive, creative, glorious, powerful, all-encompassing Love.

I leave you in peace. We are truly one with our powerful, purely loving Creator. Every action, indeed every thought, either leads to more lessons or positive construction of the Creation. Let us think, speak, and act our way to a more rapid re-emergence with our blissful home. We are on Earth to gain wisdom, be authentic, and learn continuous gratitude and unconditional love for everyone, everything, 24/7 . . . with confident, resilient, irrepressible joy every hour, every minute, every second! Blessings!!!

Dr. Jim Roach is America's Healer. His most recent book, *Brilliance – The Pursuit of Hope, Wisdom, and the Divine,* " . . . is truly a Brilliant book, produced by a brilliant and encyclopedic mind . . . one of the finest physicians in the world, in the arenas of Integrative Medicine, holistic healing, and in the true integration of spirituality and healing . . . ."

"This is the most amazing and comprehensive book I have ever read," Dwight McKee, MD.

"A sacred blending of ancient intuitive knowing, scientific prowess, and other worldly experiences . . . ," *Vital Strategies in Cancer* is one of the top integrative cancer books in the country, endorsed by multi #1 NY Times best-selling author, Mark Hyman, MD.

" . . . The most important, practical, and comprehensive (indeed, encyclopedic) book to appear in the integrative cancer area . . . ." Dwight McKee, MD.

In cancer, Dr. Roach is a published researcher and national speaker with an international clientele. Dr. Roach's book on his patients' spiritual near-death experiences, *God's House Calls,* was #1 on Amazon in four categories.

Multi NY Times #1 bestseller, Jack Canfield, author of *Chicken Soup for the Soul,* told Dr. Roach " . . . You are one of the most encyclopedic minds I have ever met," (interview at www.drroach.net).

Dr. Roach is one of the world's leading integrative medicine experts, America's top botanical physician, and #1 Amazon best-selling author in holistic medicine. Specializing in nutritional, botanical, spiritual, integrative, cancer, and holistic medicine, he hosts, and is chief presenter, for a national, annual, integrative holistic and cancer conference. "Double-boarded" in integrative medicine (ABOIM,

ABIHM), Dr. Roach has presented from Boston, to Mayo Clinic, to Los Angeles, to Houston, to Miami.

For signed copies of his books, information on his annual integrative holistic and cancer conference, or to sign up for his monthly newsletter, go to www.drroach.net.

Dr. Roach's office website is www.themidwaycenter.com.

Hear his amazing spiritual pathway:

https://www.newthinkingallowed.org/holistic-doctor . . .

Chapter 6
Fight or Flight
Beth Chase

Our spiritual journeys are full of lessons and experiences that shape us. The universe has placed, on my path, individuals and unique experiences that have taken me to higher frequencies and awakened my abilities. While I believe that we are never truly alone, we must do our own spiritual work. We must find our purpose and overcome whatever lessons lie ahead. True spiritual growth sometimes requires breaking patterns, healing, and finding forgiveness. Our thoughts have a direct impact on our well-being. It is easy to let ego take over, unless we find a way to remain connected to our Higher Self, that part of ourselves that is tethered to the Universe, the divine, to God.

My childhood was idyllic. Nestled in a small town in western Kentucky, my childhood home, once a dairy farm, sat firmly anchored in its beauty among the backdrop of magnolia and dogwood trees. The house was full of windows, which allowed for plenty of natural light to soak in. I always loved to rise early and sit in the big bay windows in the morning with our family dog, I was five years old when we moved to the home. There were areas of the house that left us all a little uncomfortable, and the living room was one of the main areas that we chose to not spend time in. It was a formal southern living room, set with antique furniture and a piano. I recall that the entire time we lived there, we entered the room as little as possible. We never entertained there. My mom would occasionally play the piano, but we kept our distance. And we never really spoke of why we avoided it. It was always cold and uninviting. It was like someone or something else was always in that room, and we were not invited.

One early morning, as I sat with our dog, I saw something I could not explain—a large black image appeared at the living room window. It was not human and it was not a costume. It had no facial features. It was not a mist, fog, or a shadow. It was unlike anything I can put into words. And it laughed in a high-pitched tone. As quickly as it appeared, it disappeared. My dog was barking at it, which validated that I did not hallucinate this image; I sat paralyzed in fear. Eventually, I mustered the energy to jump up and run to my parents' bedroom, only to be told that I was "dreaming."

I never saw the black image again, but I remember it to this day . . . vividly. It took me years to talk about it because of the fear of ever seeing it again. Over the course of my childhood, my family and I would experience frequent episodes of unexplained activity in the home. I do not particularly care to use the term "haunted," because that can evoke fear and evil. Whatever was happening, it seemed playful—later, it would turn into a protective force.

There were shadow figures, footsteps in the attic, night terrors. My friends, understandably, would not want to sleep over at my house because of strange lights, sounds, and shadows that would scare them at night. I recall my best friend, Jennifer, waking me one night as we slept in my bedroom, asking if I saw "the things" at the window. "Yes, and you'll get used to it," I casually responded. This, in hindsight, sounds like something I would say—validating and dismissing her all at the same time.

As I got older, the activity intensified. I recall having a group of friends over for a gathering one evening when my parents were away. We were around sixteen or seventeen years old. Suddenly, we overheard the piano play a few keys in the living room, perhaps four to six notes. Of course, we first thought someone was playing a joke on us, but we were all in the same room, and the sounds came from the unoccupied living room, where the piano resided. How could this be possible? But then, it happened again—four more piano keys were struck! The boys that were over at my house ran out of the house and drove off. I begged my remaining friend to stay with me until sunrise, and she reluctantly agreed, as long as we stayed awake with the television on.

The following day, I bravely went into the living room and sat at the piano. I asked whoever or whatever it was to stop scaring me, and I decided to set some ground rules. I requested that "it" only play the piano if I am in danger or my family is in danger. Was I bargaining with a ghost?

The spirit delivered on that request in the most unexpected ways.

One night my mother let our dog out to use the bathroom at midnight. My bedroom was close to the front door, and her opening the door woke me. I suddenly recall hearing her panicked voice, yelling at the dog to get back inside the house. She hollered to me that there was a truck in our driveway with what she thought to be a man getting out of the truck. We were home alone—my dad, at this point, lived out of state, and my sister was away at college.

Then it happened.

The piano played, five or six keys. I was flabbergasted . . . "it" remembered our deal! Mom had never believed me when I told her the story of the piano playing on its own, but that night, she ran past my room, exclaiming, "I believe you now!" It was warning us of danger. I could not believe it! Apparently, this spirit was intelligent. But who was it?

What did they want? I felt so vindicated that someone else in my family heard the piano play on its own.

This was a big deal!

There are so many more incidents that occurred after that, as well. Too many to cite, but I will highlight a few that merit. One profound memory and warning was when my friend called to ask me to go to Arkansas with her on a weekend trip. I told her I would think about it and would call her back. When I hung up the phone, the piano played. Again, five to six keys. I immediately took that as a sign, an omen, that I should not go with her on the trip. I called her and declined the invitation. That weekend, she and the passenger in her car were in a horrible car accident. It was so bad that they had to cut her hair just to set her free from the vehicle. I was warned, and had I not listened, I would have been in the accident, too. I started to really rely on the spirit as a protector, growing fond of whatever was there. I never felt that it was evil, malevolent, or wanted to hurt us, but I also understood that what was happening was not normal or explainable.

There were several incidents in which 911 was called from our home telephone line, even though no one ever placed the calls. The last night my mom resided in the home, the police knocked on the door at 1 a.m. due to a phone call to 911 from inside the home. This was impossible, as the landline phone service had already been disconnected days prior, in preparation for my mother's move. The police explained that the call definitely came in under the landline number, and it was a hang up. The spirit, we think, was desperate for my mom not to leave the home.

The new owner stayed in the home for approximately one year. I went to visit our old next-door neighbor a few years ago, and she told me that the new owner's personality completely transformed from kind and pleasant, to angry, dark, and threatening over the course of that single year. The house was put up for sale again. I cannot help but think that the spirit became angry that we had left and tormented the new resident, in a misguided effort to get us to come back. I feel sadness for her—I am sure she was seeking peace but instead, unknowingly found herself at the mercy of a wrathful spirit.

We never really could trace the history of the home outside of us being the third owners. The first was a doctor and his family, the second owners were still alive during my childhood experiences there, and we were the third. The land had a bigger story to tell, however, and I am not sure we will ever know its true origin.

I am sharing these deeply personal stories, with the hope that if you have experienced anything similar, you will feel unashamed, perhaps even open to sharing your own experiences. I work in a field that relies on facts and evidence. This is quite a contrast to my personal experiences. To be totally honest, I think I would be a total skeptic had I not experienced any of these things so directly. It certainly changes you when you vividly encounter the "unexplained." I ignored a lot of my abilities in college and quite frankly, there was a sense of relief that I was gone from the home. My mom started to have more personal experiences in the home after I moved away.

My fascination grew as I was in my late teenage years. I remember begging my mom to buy me books authored by Sylvia Browne. I didn't have the internet to rely on for my studies or to share my experiences with others. I wondered if I was also a "sensitive." It turns out, I am, and I didn't always see this as a gift. I have had numerous encounters with loved ones that have passed over—they have come to me through music, technology, birds, and dreams. But most of all, I am an animal empath.

Being able to understand an animal's thoughts and needs without using words is truly an incredible gift, allowing me to offer healing to them in times of illness. I spent summers on my grandparents Oklahoma ranch and learned very quickly how emotions affect animals. My granddaddy, Cowboy Corbett, had horses and cattle. I recall a lightning strike that took the life of one of the cows. I watched out the windows, afterwards; in the pasture lay the deceased cow. All of the other cows gathered around, grieving him in a circle. I felt the immense emotions from them all—they were honoring and protecting and saying goodbye.

I started meditating in 2018 and learned that, the quieter my mind, the easier it was for spirit to show up. Over time, I developed the ability to communicate with my own spirit guides. I receive messages when a spirit has something to say or seeks to provide a warning. I cannot read anyone's energy on command, however, and I'm not a palm reader or a fortune teller—I simply have an open mind and heart and a belief that we exist outside of "this" space.

I'd like to provide a word of caution here: Being prudent is as important within the spiritual community as it is in other areas of life. I have met with several mediums, and it is my belief that only one of them was truly connected to their abilities. Be wary of individuals that claim to be able to connect to your loved ones—mediumship can be a predatory business for people who are grieving. I do not think everyone is as spiritually evolved as they claim to be. In my own experience, sometimes the loudest person in the room is the one you may want to avoid.

While we all have the ability to connect to our Higher Self, be mindful that your journey and gifts can be used for healing but only when you are truly doing the work. For example, I had to learn to forgive myself, and others, at a time when it was very difficult to do so. It became an important lesson for me—solitude provided me with the time and space to let go of anger, resentment. Only in those moments, did I really grow. You can be happy and hurting at the same time. That's part of awakening.

I am grateful for my childhood experiences, because it led me to an incredible tribe of individuals with similar experiences and abilities. It has become *religion* to me to worship in the beauty of nature and soak it in as much as possible. There is nothing quite like fresh air.

Mother Earth offers us so many incredible gifts! Grounding, ice baths, sound healing, and meditation are other amazing practices to keep the mind and body in balance.

Personally, I also think it's important to balance one's life with things that are outside the spiritual realm. Find and connect with people from all walks of life. Your vibe will naturally attract your tribe. Be open and accepting of individual differences and beliefs. I would caution against trying to convince anyone to believe something just because it's part of "your" belief system. We must learn to dwell in discomfort—that is part of the journey.

One of my favorite movies is *Eat, Pray, Love*. Julia Roberts reminds me so much of myself in this film—she wants so badly to find her light. Her fellow and more experienced yogi tells her, "You have to select your thoughts in the morning, the same way that you select your clothes every day, and that is a power you can cultivate."

She replies, "I am trying!" And he quickly retorts, "That's the problem; stop trying and surrender."

Feel the shit. And surrender.

I have met a lot of good people along my path. Unexpected connections. I have had to determine if these are healthy connections. Not everyone you meet is meant to be permanent. Learn something from each of these relationships. Spending time giving back, such as volunteering at a nonprofit organization, is an act of kindness. It is so good for our souls to give towards others. Animals will connect to spiritually awakened individuals—if you take time to notice, animals sense energy faster than most people can. Trees also hold energy, as do plants, water, and things of nature. Everything is energy.

I have found value in writing, sound baths, cacao ceremonies, past life regressions, guided meditation, and hypnosis. I practice yoga and teach trauma-focused yoga to women that are struggling to find the light within. I try to interact with people from different areas of life with different belief systems. I do not at all believe in pressuring or preaching to others about any specific religion, conviction, or faith being better than another. We are all one. Although it may sound counterintuitive, a helpful way to assist another is to focus on *our own* self-improvement. After all, we are in charge or our own journey. Our guides cannot do everything for us; we have to do the work. I like to think that I respect other people's individual journeys in the process of growth and development.

We are all a collection of moments and experiences. There is no one to impress in this life but you. Shine your light. Live well and with heart.

Beth Chase is a graduate of Murray State University and has worked in the field of criminal justice for fifteen years. Beth is certified as a Trauma-Informed Yoga Instructor. She serves on the Board of Directors for a local animal and equine rescue nonprofit that serves adults and children with physical, cognitive, and social disabilities. She is most at peace living a quiet life in the country with her husband and rescuing animals.

Contact Beth at wildflowersbc@yahoo.com

Chapter 7
The Wakeup Call
Kimberly May, CFNC

"God, please help me!"

I felt an explosion. There was glass and debris everywhere, I couldn't breathe or move, I couldn't get out. I was trapped between the door and the console! The dashboard of the car was on top of me—I was completely covered in glass and fragments of the car. I didn't realize, at the time, that what I thought was the end of my life was really the beginning of a new one.

It was a beautiful, clear blue sky, a sunny kind of Sunday in late summer of 1991. My husband and I were going for a drive to the river to meet my sister and her boyfriend to go out on his boat for a day of fun. We were newlyweds, we had good jobs, and I had, just that day, found a church that I really loved. Everything looked like it was lining up to be the life of our dreams. Without warning, everything changed in the blink of an eye.

My husband and I were chatting about the day, when I noticed we had missed our turn.

"Was that where we were supposed to turn?" I asked.

We veered quickly to the left, and out of the corner of my eye, I saw a red corvette speeding quickly towards us. Before I could process what was happening, the sports car smashed directly into my car door.

"God! You have to help me now!"

At that moment, it felt as if God picked me up and held me in the arms of love. I felt no pain . . . only peace, joy, love, calm, and complete expansiveness. I felt connected to everything and everyone. It was such an amazing feeling of bliss! I felt like I was home in this beautiful light of oneness. I wanted to move closer to those feelings and towards divinity. It was a wonderful feeling, and I didn't ever want to leave it!

But I heard, *"It's not your time."*

I realized I was hovering over the car and the scene of the accident. I could see the ambulance, fire trucks, police cars, and the people who had gathered around to observe the crash. My sister, who was still waiting for me at the boat dock, received a call over a loudspeaker about the accident.

I recall watching the rescue of our bodies from above the car. The vehicle had rolled down into a ravine, and my body was trapped between the console and the passenger side door. My husband had hit his head and was unconscious. The paramedics used the Jaws of Life to try to get me out of the car, but it didn't work; they decided to cut the roof off the car. Placing a board under my legs, they skillfully lifted me out of the top of the car. I was jolted back into my body, only to feel the tremendous pain of my broken left femur, right arm, and elbow. It was shocking to be back in my body, and I was in agony!

The people on the scene of the accident said there was absolutely no explanation for my miraculous survival, given the damage to the car. The circulating story was that the girl in the car had died. I was transported to the hospital in a helicopter, and I sang hymns to myself all the way there. I couldn't believe I was alive! When I got to the hospital the chaplain went out to tell my worried family that I was alive and well. My husband was at the same hospital but in a separate room. Although we couldn't see each other at first, we were able to speak by phone. He had internal bleeding and was released a few days later. I was in the hospital for two weeks, however, having surgeries to install a metal rod in my left femur, as well as two plates and thirteen screws in my right arm to repair it.

People would tell me, "I am praying for you all." And I could *feel* it in my body, in the room, and in my heart. I *knew* I would be healed. Yet, I started to question everything. Why was I still here? What was I supposed to do? Why did this happen to me? Where was that peaceful place I visited and how could I get back there?

My old life didn't seem to fit me anymore. I felt out of place. Meaningless activities and conversations were no longer fulfilling, perhaps because I should have died but I didn't . . . I knew it wasn't my time. I had come to realize that I was not my body, that I was infinite. At a deeper level, this knowledge removed all my fears and changed my belief systems. The knowledge that there was so much more to our lives and existence now colored all my interactions. I wanted so much more out of life!

However, I began to experience horrible claustrophobia. Having been trapped in my vehicle during the accident, it was difficult to be in a car or any small space. Figuring out an imaginary evacuation plan became a new routine. Yet part of me had no fear at all, because *I knew I was more than my physical body*. Nevertheless, I had a tough time staying in mine.

Since I had left my body and traveled to such a blissful, peaceful place, I kept wanting to go back there. I couldn't make sense of it all, at only twenty-seven years old. I visited my internal medicine doctor and told him about my near-death experience (NDE).

"Do you want to be here?" he asked.

"That's a good question," I said. "It's hard to be back here. There's so much pain."

My orthopedic doctor had advised me that I may not get full mobility back in my right arm and elbow. I was in a wheelchair and couldn't use my right arm or left leg. I started asking myself questions: *Why am I here? What is my purpose? What is life for? How can I experience more joy?*

A guy from church offered his services for healing with energy work, a practice called Reiki. I didn't know what it was, but he suggested, "If it doesn't help, you don't have to pay for it." So I had nothing to lose. He even made a house call! The Reiki session really helped me to relax and feel better; it even relieved the pain.

When I went back to my orthopedic doctor, he asked, "What are you doing? You're healing so quickly!"

I told him about the Reiki sessions, my daily practices, and my NDE experience. His response was, "You were in shock, and I am not sure about the other stuff." Although he was a great doctor, I felt like he didn't believe me. I thought to myself, *I shouldn't talk about this to other people.*

During my recovery, I visualized my body healing, prayed for guidance, journaled, received Reiki healing sessions, and continued with my physical therapy. Being present with the pain, knowing I'd get past the pain, and remembering that I was *more* than the pain really accelerated my love for my body and focused my life. I started researching how to heal the body and how to use your mind to heal yourself and create the life you want.

A part of me wanted to get back to work and return to a "normal" life. I tried to go back to my corporate recruiting job on a walker, but my boss said, "No, you need to heal up first; however, you can start making calls from home." I did as he suggested, but it felt meaning-less, even though everyone was encouraging me to get back to my old life. I felt like a fish out of water; the things I used to do felt empty. I wanted more of the feelings I experienced on the other side. How could I get more of those blissful feelings? I eventually went back to work but it was not fulfilling to me.

I wanted to be my authentic Self; it felt like it was the most important thing I could do. I even found a picture of a woman from a CD cover that looked a little like me . . . a bit older, but she looked authentic, healthy, joyful, and happy. "How can I be more like this?" I asked. I kept her picture on my bulletin board and looked at it each day, visu-alizing myself fully healed, with full mobility in all my joints, joyfully helping *others* live their lives to their fullest potential. I would pray/meditate, write about it, draw pictures of it, make vision boards, listen to motivational speakers, talk to people who had done the same . . . any way I could find to get closer to the life I knew I was meant to live but wasn't.

Then I was laid off from my job.

What an unexpected gift that was! I would write in the mornings with my non-dominant hand, which for me is my left hand. This process is supposed to override your ego, get you into your heart, and uncover what you really want. The question I would ask is, "What is my highest aspiration that I came to fulfill?"

Subsequently, a nurse who trained at Duke that I went to church with offered Reiki training, and I knew I wanted to train with her. This was a big turning point for me—I have been using and providing Reiki treatments since then.

I continued to journal, determined to manifest my dream job. Here is one of my journal entries from around that time—at the time of this entry, I was still in the corporate world, but I really wanted to work in the wellness field.

Thank you, God, for placing me in the right place to use my skills. I know you are guiding me to my divine purpose.

Job Description: Using Reiki and other tools to help others and myself to release illness and past problems. Use my healing abilities combined with art to inspire people to let go of the past, share my story through motivational speaking. My purpose is to help others to see the divine in themselves and others. To be an example, healer, artist, teacher, motivational public speaker. Please help me to use my voice to lift others in love, hope and promise. To bring out the best in others.

One morning, I saw a small newspaper ad for a public speaker at a two-year college. I interviewed for the position and got it. The job was going to high schools and talking to students about their future. I drove all over rural Kentucky, before I had GPS, so I got lost a lot! But I sure had a good time talking to students and encouraging them to follow their dreams, and I got to practice my public speaking skills. This was before PowerPoint, and we used slides on a projector.

One of the slides was a bit of an optical puzzle that could be seen two ways: a beautiful young lady or an old woman. I still have trouble finding the old woman in the picture because my eyes so intensely focus on the young lady, but I know other people who see the old woman easily. It's funny how our minds play these tricks on us, isn't it? It illustrated how to change your perspective and see things differently. I knew we created our reality with our thoughts, words, and intentions. This was my favorite presentation, and I knew I wanted to do more of it! "Your word is your wand," I'd tell the students, and I absolutely believe this today.

Love What You Do, Do What You Love

For years, I wrote about my dream job: to help others to be healthy and more joyful, to relax, listen to their heart and be more authentic. I made vision boards, talked to mentors, and attended classes in health and wellness. By then, I had returned to the corporate world, as a marketing manager for an international fast-food company. I was doing everything I said I wanted to do in college. But now it was making me sick and unfulfilled. I recognized that I could not sell my soul and life's purpose any longer, no matter the money I was earning and despite everyone around me urging me to stay in my good, solid job with a 401K and benefits.

I prayed and meditated for guidance and direction, knowing that I would be guided on how to share with people that they are infinitely loved and that each has their own unique purpose. I escaped to a destination spa that had an integrative clinic and bed and breakfast on a beautiful, thirteen-thousand-acre farm with horses and gardens. I would go there and *"get it back to good,"* as I called it. Then I would go back to work and dream of being back on the farm. Occasionally, I would call to ask if they needed marketing assistance, but they would say, "No, we have a marketing director." I persevered, asking anyway.

Then one day, I went to a transformational seminar about creating a new future and putting the past in the past. I created the possibility of being courageous! When I arrived home, everything looked and felt different. I went back to work the next day and wrote my resignation letter, stating I wanted to make a bigger difference in the world, use my true gifts, and be my authentic Self. I knew in the end I would regret continuing the path I was on. But I knew that's not what I came here to do, and I needed to get on with my real-life purpose.

The people at work who knew me best gave me a going away party with a gift basket containing a mug, which read, *Love what you do, do what you Love.* The purple and white cup, which I still have today, is one of my favorite things. I cherish it because it explains my true feelings and what I really wanted to do at that time. I started asking the question, "What would a courageous person do?" And then, I *did* those things—I made a list of all the places around me that offered holistic health, and I went to those places to see if they would hire me.

I succeeded! I went from working in fast food, to attaining my dream job: marketing manager for that same wellness spa and integrative clinic. I had manifested a new career path, and I was earning even more money than I had at my corporate job! It was there that I healed my body from all the damage I incurred while working in fast food. But I still found myself stressed and running at the same pace as in my previous job. The doctor at the wellness spa explained that I needed to manage my stress differently and suggested I learn Heart-Math®, which helps people to manage their emotions and behaviors to reduce stress, increase resilience, and tap into their natural intuitive guidance.

I trained in HeartMath® and started listening to my heart. It helped me to deal with my grief from a lot of personal losses, as well as stress and health issues; afterwards, I began to help others to do the same. In my role at the wellness spa, I gave presentations to corporate groups, while continuing to train in many other healing modalities, eventually becoming a health coach and licensed HeartMath® provider and Reiki Master teacher. I got to live my dream there for over six years!

Then, one day, I signed up for a free life coaching session and told the coach that I wanted to start my own coaching business. She said, "What if you could do it now?" She coached me on how to move through what was stopping me . . . mostly fear of putting myself out there and moving forward. Interestingly, the very next week, we had a companywide meeting, and they announced that the wellness clinic was closing! I was shocked and scared about venturing out on my own to start my own business, but I realized I was getting exactly what I asked for in my coaching session.

Later, I trained in the Havening Techniques® and was able to heal my claustrophobia. The rest is history, as they say. I started my own business, called Inspire Wellness, to inspire and breathe life into others, to help them ignite the fire within and find their soul's purpose. I proudly share my NDE and what I learned from it—that you are an infinite spirit, you are loved, you *are* love . . . only love remains. Listen to your inner voice and be your authentic Self. You are unique and all you need to do is just *be you*! You really can't mess it up—these are all lessons you came to learn. Relax into and surrender to the flow of life and the divine creator. We are all connected.

For me, going inward was my way out. Listening to my inner voice, trusting it, and making time to be still and practice gratitude. Peace is just a breath away. I now live the life of my dreams! I love what I do, and I do what I love!!

"Love what you do and do what you love. Don't listen to anyone else who tells you not to do it. You do what you want, what you love. Imagination should be the center of your life."
— Ray Bradbury

"Find the place inside yourself where nothing is impossible."
— Deepak Chopra

Kimberly May is a Wellness Coaching Specialist, Certified Havening Techniques® Practitioner, Licensed HeartMath® Provider, Functional Nutrition Counselor, and Reiki Master teacher with twenty-five years' experience working in the Wellness field—as both a business owner and wellness professional for five integrative health centers. After burning out from the corporate world, she refocused her energy on getting back to the basics—growing her own food, cooking nutritious meals, and learning to listen to her inner voice and act on it. She loves coaching others to reach their full potential and optimal well-being, align with their life purpose, reduce stress, and remove blocks to their authentic Self. She spends her free time enjoying organic gardening, cooking, dancing, creating art, traveling, and teaching others how to live a healthy, authentic life that they love!

Contact Kimberly at www.inspirewellness.net

Chapter 8
I See You!
Judy Buchanan, LTC, Ret

"I see you!" I said to myself.

When I was seven years old, I stood in front of my parents' bedroom full length mirror looking deeply into the expanse of my blue eyes. At that moment, I saw my soul. I had a profound epiphany that my divine essence, my infinite soul, was inside the little body I saw in the mirror. I thought to myself, *How am I in this body?* The statement, "The eyes are the windows to the soul," was true for me at that moment. As I looked at myself, a sense of awe overtook me. I now believe this is the essence of what we call, "awakening." *Awakening* is remembering that your consciousness, the real you, is divinely connected to the infinite energy of God/Source and there is so much more to life than just a limited physical existence.

My lifelong journey of pondering who I am and why I am here began that day, but it was not until my late thirties that I diligently explored these questions. Like many others, I experienced several moments of awakening throughout my life, which revealed to me that I am a multidimensional consciousness of infinite light energy that has incarnated into a variety of physical forms within multiple timelines.

I am so grateful that I have decided to incarnate once again as a human on this amazing planet Earth to experience the exciting and challenging rollercoaster of life in all its beauty.

At twenty-nine days old, I was adopted by two wonderful humans. My parents, Tom and Carol, had decided to adopt a child after trying to conceive for several years, unsuccessfully. After they made the decision to adopt me, they became pregnant with my sister, Patty. Patty was born just seven months and twenty-two days later. Within four years, my youngest sister, Cindy, was born. Being adopted gave me another level of curiosity to question, *Who am I?* Growing up, I had no knowledge about my biological family, so I often wondered about my heritage. I was raised Catholic, my mother's religion, but my father was Protestant. My father had his own way of connecting with spirituality, demonstrating to me that it was perfectly acceptable to have varying beliefs in our family. It was clear to me that love and support did not hinge on all of us embracing the exact same understanding about life and our spiritual essence.

Becoming acutely and chronically ill in my thirties caused me to question my beliefs regarding life and my spiritual essence. Physical pain and discomfort were the major contributing factors to my awakening process and have facilitated a complete transformation of who I know I am. I endured six surgeries and have been diagnosed with many gastrointestinal issues, including gastro-esophageal reflux disease and irritable bowel syndrome, along with heart palpitations, anemia, uterine fibroids, ovarian cysts, cervical dysplasia, chronic joint pain, plantar fasciitis in both feet, vertigo, and panic attacks.

Being an active-duty Medical Service Corps Officer in the United States Army Medical Department, I was inclined to follow the western medical model. While I do believe western medical health care can be extraordinarily helpful and lifesaving, especially when working with physical trauma, I was not getting the results I needed just by taking drugs and working with my physical body as prescribed. The root cause of the chronic pain and discomfort that I was experiencing was not being addressed. So pain was my catalyst for change! This is when I took the leap to begin to explore holistic healing practices.

Exploring Holistic Practices

You never know who might have a message that will change your life. One day after having my teeth cleaned, I was chatting with a military dental hygienist about the excruciating abdominal pain, dizziness and panic attacks I was experiencing, and she suggested I see an acupuncturist to assist in resolving my issues. This was not an option inside the military at the time, so I was grateful she recommended her acupuncturist, someone she knew and trusted. Acupuncture is a technique for balancing the flow of energy or life force (chi). Chi flows through meridians or pathways in your body. By inserting needles into specific points along these meridians, acupuncture practitioners facilitate opening these channels so your energy flow will re-balance and support healing.

In 2010, I met my first acupuncturist, Dr. Bastress, who is a Sufi leader. Sufism is the esoteric or mystical aspect of Islam. The aim of Sufi practice is to gain direct knowledge of the eternal in this life. Little did I know that Dr. Bastress would not only help me physically, but also mentally, emotionally, and spiritually. I learned that pain is not just a facet of the physical being but can be a combination of imbalance with the mental, emotional, and spiritual aspects of Self. I now understand that I am a whole person, and I cannot separate parts of myself to treat just one part, i.e. the physical aspect, and expect to fully heal.

Perhaps like many of you, I have been through a variety of traumatic experiences in life. What I didn't realize was that I was holding on to the energy and chemistry of those past traumatic experiences. Army training had taught me to push through pain, suck it up, and drive on. I became very good at enduring high levels of pain and stuffing my feelings, especially at work. Driven by this training, I kept moving forward without addressing any of the emotional, mental or spiritual pain of the past. Eventually, though, my body forced me to stop and get help.

In time, I realized that not only was I dealing with a health crisis, I was also living through a spiritual one. The belief that I was going to hell for all the mistakes I made was ingrained in me by my Catholic upbringing, leading to dissonance within. An example of this internal turmoil was the guilt I felt for having to leave my children, often, for work throughout their young lives. One of the most difficult periods of separation was when I deployed for a year to Southwest Asia in support of Operation Iraqi Freedom (OIF). I was able to return home on R&R for two weeks midway through my deployment. Although it was wonderful to be home with my husband and children, returning to the battlefield and leaving my children again was even more heart wrenching than when I had initially deployed. It was so emotionally intense and challenging on my body, mind, and spirit that I became immediately ill with heart palpitations, gastrointestinal issues and dizziness. The battlefield physician on staff decided it was best to give me a prescription to put me to sleep for two days so I could recalibrate to being on duty again. This experience is one of numerous emotional, physical, and mental traumas I had sustained throughout my life, had not yet processed, and was still held in my body. The traumas I had survived were affecting my present life, because I had not yet allowed myself the opportunity and resources to come to peace with them.

Working with this acupuncturist provided the first opportunity to begin letting go of limiting beliefs around who I am. One day, he asked if he could do a form of spiritual cleansing instead of acupuncture. I love trying new things, so I said, "Yes, let's do it." That energetic purification experience was one of the most profound spiritual experiences of my life! During the appointment, I laid on the table, just as I did for my regular acupuncture sessions. For the next hour or so, I lost track of time. He simply held his hands above my body with no contact as he prayed out loud in Arabic with prayers from the *Music of the Soul* Sufi teachings text.

As he prayed words I could not understand, I began to feel pain rise from deep within me. I started to cry and then sob while my body shook and writhed with pain. I could feel pain move across my entire body and change the positions it occupied during the session. As soon as one pain spot was alleviated, another part of my body experienced pain. Eventually, as I continued to allow the flow of energy, I could feel all the pain leaving my body through my feet. My body, mind, and spirit settled into a remarkable sense of pain-free peace. When the process was complete, I felt so clear, light, joyous and connected. For the first time in my life, I could feel God/Source energy pulsing through me. This sensation of direct connection to God/Source was magnificent! This experience aided me in knowing myself as an expansive spiritual Being having a physical experience of life.

To understand what had just occurred, I began to dive deeper into learning about different aspects of spirituality. The second doorway of awakening opened when I read *Journey of Souls - Case Studies of Life Between Lives* by Michael Newton. I grew up with the belief that you only live one life for all eternity. This book intrigued me and opened my consciousness to the concept of reincarnation. Desiring more insight and understanding I read a plethora of spiritual and self-help books helping me to view and embrace different perspectives.

The Issues Live in the Tissues

My adult life, as a mother, wife and active-duty Army soldier, has always been very busy. As it is for many in our society, life was go, go, go and don't stop. I believed that it was my obligation to perform successfully, all the time, at the highest level in every area of my life. I learned to constantly keep my nervous system on alert. This eventually caused my body to experience anxiety and then panic attacks along with many other health issues I have previously described.

When I retired from military service in 2012, I was dealing with unbearable plantar fasciitis in both feet and debilitating shoulder pain. It was time to help my body, mind and spirit heal from the years of bodily abuse I subjected myself to while in the Army. This is when I decided to try massage therapy.

Aldene is a massage and craniosacral therapist who is very intuitive. She helped me to reconnect with my body after years of disconnecting from it. As we collaborated to facilitate my healing, I learned from direct somatic experience that "Our issues live in our tissues." Our struggles can live on in our physical being long after an event has occurred. They can be held in our body, mind and spirit until we feel safe enough to allow the energy and chemistry of the event to rise again to be transformed. After six months of diligent work together, she suggested I see a Reiki practitioner. This was the third doorway of awakening opening to take me on a journey to know the depths of my soul.

Having no idea what Reiki was, I decided to trust the advice of Aldene and try it. Reiki is a Japanese holistic, non-invasive, deep relaxation energy medicine treatment. This treatment involves light touch or no touch, and its purpose is to reduce stress, pain, and tension while jumpstarting a person's innate self-healing mechanisms. The day I had my first Reiki session, I was experiencing pain in my shoulders. While the practitioner, Susan, was holding her hands lightly on me and above me, I could feel the energy moving in my body and my pain being alleviated. As soon as I was off the table, I knew I needed to learn this healing modality. Within a month, I took my first Reiki class, and this propelled me to even greater levels of metaphysical exploration and experience. Since 2013, I have taken numerous courses that involve different forms of energy medicine and yoga. It has been a constant discovery process filled with exciting "Aha!" moments and divinely orchestrated connections.

Souls are Multidimensional Infinite Energy

Along my path of spiritual discovery and healing, I took a three-day class with Brian L. Weiss, M.D., author of the book *Many Lives, Many Masters,* to experience past life hypnotic regression. After this experience, I knew I wanted to explore this modality further, and within a short period of time, I met Cathie, a hypnotherapist. We became instant friends. She and I would go on to spend several years trading sessions with each other so I could explore other lifetime experiences via hypnosis, and she could experience transformation through energy medicine. Eventually, I became Beyond Quantum Healing (BQH) Hypnosis trained myself. All these experiences solidified my truth: that I am a multidimensional Being who has incarnated in countless timelines and will continue to do so, for infinity. I believe not only have our souls incarnated on other timelines but in lots of different types of bodies throughout the universe. For most of my life I had not allowed my consciousness to expand to this cosmic understanding due to conditioned fear around the existence of extraterrestrials; that is, until there were significant personal events that facilitated that exploration.

I have always been emphatically sensitive (an empath). I can feel the emotions and energy of others, and I often seem to know accurate information that simply comes into my awareness. Later in my life, I learned that these abilities are called clairsentience (clear feeling) and claircognizance (clear knowing). As a child, I remember being scared to go to sleep at night, because I felt energy and/or Beings in my room. My parents always reassured me it was safe to go to sleep, but that didn't eliminate the feeling that something was there with me. As I continued my Reiki practice and exploration into a variety of different holistic healing modalities, my senses heightened, and I discovered that this practice facilitated even more mystical and extraordinary experiences.

One evening in late summer of 2015, I was driving alone near my home. As I was about to make a left-hand turn onto a country road, I saw—just above the tree line—approximately fifteen, equally-spaced, brilliant white lights that were hovering in a semi-circle almost directly above me. These solid white lights extended beyond the road on both sides. I did a double take and asked myself, *out loud*, "Am I really seeing this?" An Unidentified Flying Object (UFO) was suspended just above and in front of me. In shock at what I was witnessing, I decided I wasn't going to tell anyone, because I thought they would think I was nuts. Little did I know, the very next day would bring yet another surprise. While driving that same road the morning after seeing the UFO, I noticed a mini crop circle on the side of a hill in the mature wheat field near where I had seen the UFO! I couldn't believe what I was seeing. I tucked this information away within me, knowing what I experienced but without any means of deciphering what had occurred.

Years later when a close friend began to channel, I decided it was time to get some answers, so I asked about this experience. A channel is a person who consciously opens to receive and translate nonphysical information from the quantum field. My suspicion was confirmed that I did indeed see a UFO manned by cosmic Beings that night, and the crop circle served as a key, placed specifically for me to unlock my consciousness to embrace the cosmic realm. Since then, through hypnosis and other metaphysical experiences, I've come to realize that I have been visited numerous times throughout my life, by a variety of multidimensional cosmic Beings. It was nice to receive validation that there was energy and/or Beings in my room at night as a child, since I could feel them but not see them.

Then in 2020, not only did I feel energy in my room at night, but I began seeing holographic energy outlines of these Beings with my eyes open! Never knowing when this might happen, I have since been woken up out of sleep many times after midnight and before 4:00 a.m. by a sound, sparks of light, a touch to my body, or vibrational sensations. I was initially fearful and confused when I was awakened, but over time, I have become more comfortable with these types of experiences. I believe these visitations are purposeful to assist me with my soul's mission to be of service to humanity.

As we move as a collective human race from being a global community to an intergalactic one, I believe we will need to continue to open our hearts and consciousnesses to embrace the understanding that all Beings in this universe are derived from and connected to one God/Source. What each of us believes or what we designate as our truth is a combination of what we are taught and what we experience. Throughout my life, my truth and beliefs have certainly changed. It has been a phenomenal journey to gain incredible insight about myself and the universe in which we live. I have awakened through continuous education and lived experience. What has propelled me forward to discover the various facets of my soul essence has been my desire to answer the question, *Who am I?* This spark was ignited within me when I saw my soul in my eyes so many years ago.

What do *you* see when you look into your eyes?

Judy Buchanan's passion is to inspire you to co-create a new reality in which you can thrive! As an energy medicine practitioner/teacher (Reiki), yoga instructor, and transformation guide, Judy creates a container of comfort providing you with the keys to awaken your inner wisdom and jumpstart your innate ability to heal and transform.

As a retired United States Army Lieutenant Colonel married to a former soldier, she understands, first-hand, the stressors experienced by first responders/service members and their families. While serving in uniform and raising a family, Judy endured multiple surgeries and experienced chronic stress, anxiety, and pain. From these health challenges came the strength and passion to spark a change that led her to explore and study numerous holistic healing and metaphysical practices.

Over the years, she has focused much of her training and certifications on the subtle energy systems of the body, nervous system regulation, and yoga. Judy uses these skills to facilitate clients' healing, awakening and transformation via one-on-one sessions, retreats, and group instruction. In 2018, wanting to share all that she had learned with those who run toward danger, Judy developed and implemented a resiliency training program for her local police academy. In addition, she holds a Master's Degree in Business Administration and a Bachelor's Degree in Social Work.

Connect with Judy and learn more about her services and resources at www.judy-buchanan.com

Chapter 9
My Journey to Enlightenment
Reverend Willis G. Polk, Sr

In my initial review and reflection on my journey, I delved deeply into my distant past, all the way back to at least age five. Through this reflection, I was able to recognize distinct "age-stages" that clearly marked my journey.

As you read my story and my journey, keep in mind that it is deeply rooted in the Black religious church tradition and all of its practices and beliefs. Ironically, these deeply ingrained traditions were some of the greatest barriers to my surrender, freedom, and enlightenment, particularly during the Turning Point stage.

I invite you to walk with me through these stages, reflecting on your own journey as we explore the profound transformations that have shaped our paths. Let us embark together on this journey of discovery and spiritual awakening.

Early Awareness—Yet Unexplainable: Ages 1–18

This period was characterized by an unexplainable presence that I could not escape or understand. It felt like living under a cloud that began to pick up weight.

For where I am today, I know that my "enlightenment" did not occur in one single moment. It clearly evolved over many years, dating as far back as age five. At that age, who really knows anything? Over all these years, I've learned that it can take almost a lifetime for us to allow God—the divine—to be who God truly is in our lives.

As I look back at those early years, I realize we often experience God as mystery. Richard Rohr, in his book *A Spring Within Us*, describes mystery as something we do not understand, cannot understand, that which is unfamiliar, and something we are not used to. This characterizes my first Age-Stage towards enlightenment.

In this stage, I was enveloped in confusion, darkness, and plenty of uncertainty. During those early years, I don't recall being able to talk with anyone about the "unexplainable," this great mystery that was upon me; there was no one to explain what I was experiencing or how I may have been behaving.

All of this had a profound impact on my thinking, which in turn, influenced my behavior and made me feel and act a bit odd compared to my peers. I think I can truly say that I was under the "mighty hand of God" more than I realized, as the Apostle Peter describes in 1 Peter 5:6-7.

It felt as though I was living under a cloud that seemed to grow heavier with time. This persistent uneasiness simply became a part of my life, something I learned to live with. I did not have the language or the understanding to describe it. But looking back after all these years, I think I can say that I was under the protective care of the divine, who was leading, guiding, and shaping my life without my knowledge. This is reminiscent of Jacob's realization after he wrestled with the divine all night.

As a child, I professed a belief in God and believed that Christ died for my sins. I had a childlike prayer life and remember talking to God in prayer. However, the church I grew up in never addressed any of what I was experiencing and never gave me the opportunity to express and explain my struggle.

So I went on to school, played sports, played music, was very social, and provided leadership in various ways, not being able to describe what was going on in private.

The Vacation Period: Ages 19–22

During this time, I thought the unexplainable presence had passed me by. It was a brief respite, where I attempted to escape from the ever-present sense of something greater.

I had to include this period to provide context for the journey. After nearly eighteen years of being enveloped in this great "mystery" that held me, restricted me, confused me, and filled me with such uncertainty, it finally seemed to have lifted. Yes, it seemed to have *gone away.*

In that, I felt a freedom that I had not experienced before. I was free—free to go, free to run and to jump, free to be merry, and free to chase all of my hunches and urges. And boy, oh boy, did I do that!

I had already graduated from high school a year ahead of my class. I got a job . . . a pretty good job. I bought a car. I had a girlfriend, played music, shot pool, joined clubs and organizations, played softball, got married and divorced. With all of this going on in the late '60s and early '70s, I listened to Curtis Mayfield and all of the Motown sounds. This was a time when the weekends were never long enough and the music was never loud enough. Many people would call this "sowing my wild oats," and they would be correct!

However, in January of the year I was to turn twenty-three, that "thing" that once had me—it not only came back upon me, but it returned with a vengeance and was now *inside* me! It had me where I could barely breathe, barely function. My vacation had come to an end. I felt in my heart it was a do-or-die situation. The summons was to get it straight and do it right.

The Great Transition—Filled with Uncertainty: Ages 23–35

This period marked the beginning of my journey towards where I am now. It was a time of seeking, searching, wondering, wandering, and pondering.

My vacation had ended, and my stay away was no more. I was back under the unexplainable weight that I had learned to live with since age five. It felt like I was under arrest, and I knew it. This time, the burden pressed and overwhelmed me in a way I hadn't experienced before. But now, I was able to seek help. The first person I thought to talk to was my pastor. Did that help? Yes. But I still resisted and hesitated. Finally, when I could no longer resist or delay, in April, 1974, I went through the Baptist protocol for admission to the Gospel Ministry.

The acknowledgment and surrender were earth-shaking, as if mountains quaked. My whole script was flipped from the inside out. Today, some would call that a "kundalini" experience. Nothing remained the same. I felt redeemed, transformed, convicted, and converted. I experienced peace, joy, and happiness. I gave myself fully and completely to the religious practices of the Christian ministry—teaching, preaching, and pastoring.

All of this became my life focus. I lived and had my being in that newness, finding clarity, direction, passion, love, and strength to do the right thing.

During this period, I embraced the rigorous path of ministry. The first five years were dedicated to study, preparation, watching, observing, and learning. I immersed myself in comparative religious studies at Simmons Bible College when I first started. That captivated my interest. The various religious practices and their pathways intrigued me, and I wanted to understand where these pathways led. (Unbeknownst to me, there was something in those practices that caught my attention that I will talk about later.)

Additionally, my introduction to mythology and philosophy demanded deep and thoughtful engagement. This intellectual pursuit continued even as I began my first pastorate. I was driven with much passion, delving deep into my ministry work. This dedication proved effective in the lives of our church membership and the community we served. We developed numerous projects, programs, and activities that attracted many to join us, particularly between 1979 and 1985.

However, shortly into my first pastorate, I faced a significant adjustment. The initial fervor and energy that had propelled me seemed to dissipate. I entered a season as mysterious as my first eighteen years of life. Today, some would call that a "dry patch" or a "dry season." My well, like the Prophet Elijah's brook, dried up (as described in 1 Kings 17:8). The challenge to continue was a real burden, one that exceeded anything I had studied at Simmons Bible College, Georgetown College, or Lexington Theological Seminary. My Baptist framework offered no guidance for this season. I struggled to make my spiritual evolution fit into my Black Baptist traditions and practices, but I couldn't.

I tugged along for about another two years, trying to make do, but it just did not work. After much prayer and consideration, I resigned from my position. This period marked a crucial transition in my journey, where I had to reconcile my spiritual experiences with the practical realities of ministry. For the next three years, I turned aside to explore this season I was in.

The Turning Point—A Major Shift: Ages 36–39

This period brought a major shift in my life, revealing things I had never known. It marked a turning inward, rather than aside, and intro-

duced me to spiritual practices beyond my traditional Christian beliefs.

During this period, I began to notice parallels between my current experiences and those from my earlier years. The tone, texture, feelings, and thoughts were strikingly similar, but now I had the maturity to better understand them. I recognized this kinship as a deeper extension of my journey.

After resigning from my first church, a dear Catholic friend introduced me to the concept of spiritual formation. She suggested that I might be experiencing what St. John of the Cross described as "the dark night of the soul." Though I was aware of his work, I had not connected it with my own struggles. She arranged a meeting with Father Hank Kenny, a Jesuit priest who had recently arrived in Lexington, Kentucky from South Africa. Upon our very first meeting, it was evident that he understood my spiritual landscape in a profound way.

One of my greatest challenges was reconciling my unique and profound metaphysical experiences with my "Baptist framework." I realized I needed to let go of my rigid adherence to Baptist traditions and open myself to new spiritual practices.

Over the next three years, Father Kenny guided me on a deep and transformative journey. He introduced me to the spiritual exercises of St. Ignatius of Loyola, which resonated deeply and provided a clear path forward. About three months into our sessions, I experienced what felt like a "portal" opening within me (akin to the portal Jesus speaks of in John 10:1-3). This subtle and graceful moment was significant and would deeply influence the final stage of my journey. Reflecting on it, I realized that if I had been pastoring at the time, I might have missed this pivotal experience.

Through Father Kenny's guidance, I learned how to reach, be in, and abide in this new spiritual state. I remained with *the portal*. This understanding has profoundly impacted everything I do. The works of St. Ignatius, Thomas Merton, and St. John of the Cross, along with other Jesuit writers, became integral to my spiritual practice.

From that point on, my journey was characterized by practice, sacrifice, discipline, perseverance, delight, and love. These elements became the foundation of my ongoing spiritual growth and enlightenment.

The Journey Onward—Yet Inward: Ages 39–47

During this time, a whole new outlook was established within me. I began to experience the divine in a very real way, guided by the teachings of St. Ignatius of Loyola, St. John of the Cross, and Thomas Merton. This period was transformative, leading me to deeper spiritual practices.

The fifth stage of my journey, from ages thirty-nine to forty-seven, was marked by a profound *inward* turn rather than a mere turning aside. This period was a significant discovery that has remained real to me for the past twenty-five years. The journey I embarked on was not across geography but a spiritual, inward journey. I caught this revelation around the age of thirty-six or thirty-seven, while I was not pastoring. I realized that had I been fully occupied with pastoral duties and responsibilities, I would have been too distracted to notice this crucial shift. The pastoral distractions would have been overwhelming.

The entrance "into" this spiritual way is very narrow, and few find it. I recognize the tremendous blessing of my spiritual guide, Father Hank Kenny, as a gift from the Universe. There is a saying that when the student is ready, the teacher will appear. This kind of spiritual guidance, with its unique aim and purpose, was not found in my Black religious tradition and cultural foundation. The practices, vocabulary, images, and depth of thought were entirely new to me.

During this period, the "lift-off" and advancement in my spiritual journey were great and glorious. I began to experience God, the divine, and the Source in ways I had never thought possible. I learned how to get there and how to BE there. My studies of St. Ignatius of Loyola, St. John of the Cross, and the works of Thomas Merton were instrumental in this phase. They kept me moving upward and onward, into the deeper things of the divine.

My devotional time with the scriptures took on a more meditative approach. I began to see the scriptures as a privileged place to experience the divine. This practice truly met my deepest spiritual needs. The writings and practices of these spiritual masters guided me into a richer, more profound experience of the divine Presence. Metaphorical and metaphysical treatments of the scriptures became a constant practice for me.

In this inward journey, I found a sense of peace and fulfillment that transcended my previous experiences. It was a journey of deepening faith, where the mysteries of the divine became more accessible and real. The inward turn was not just a phase but a lifelong path that has continued to shape and guide my spiritual journey.

Spiritual Formation and Persistence: Ages 48–73

At this point, I had developed a true spiritual formation that cultivated my spiritual landscape. This period was marked by persistence, personal sacrifice, discipline, and perseverance. It allowed me to persist with intentionality, leading to a greater enlightenment that transcended my traditional religious practices.

Over time, I learned to really work on the "Process." I saw that there is honestly a method to "the madness." For me it was meditation, deep meditation. I had to really learn and practice humility, obedience, sacrifice, discipline, perseverance and steadfastness. I had to learn to recognize the presence and the voice of the divine. In the later years, I expanded my exploration to include practices like Reiki, yoga, and singing bowls, as well as the study of frequency, sacred geometry, vibration, nature, and patterns. In my journey, the path of enlightenment was gradual, truly taking a lifetime. But I was so thankful I stayed the course. The Bible says, "Ask and it shall be given unto you, seek and ye shall find, knock, and the door shall be open unto you" (Matthew 7:7-11).

My friends, *stay the course*.
Peace, love and happiness.

Rev. Willis Polk, Sr. was born and raised in Versailles, Kentucky. He entered the "Christian Preaching Ministry" in May, 1974.

He graduated High School from Woodford County High School in 1968 and studied for the ministry at Kentucky State University, Simmons Bible College, Georgetown College in Georgetown, Kentucky, and Lexington Theological Seminary. He studied in the fields of religion, psychology, and church administration.

Rev Polk pastored at First Baptist Church, Versailles, Kentucky from 1979–1985, Antioch Baptist Church, Lexington, Kentucky from 1989–1996, and Imani Baptist Church, Lexington, Kentucky from 1997–2024.

He was tutored in Spirituality with Father Hank Kenny in the practice of St. Ignatius in 1986. This relationship spanned twenty-five years. Rev. Polk has studied spirituality with a focus on contemplative prayer along with metaphysical and metaphorical interpretation of the Bible. He has taught prayer formation and discipleship for thirty years. He has nearly twenty-five thousand hours of study, research and writing in this area of study.

Rev. Polk says, in his fifty years of work, he has found that a consistent prayer life and study of God's word is the greatest struggle for most church going individuals. At this point in his ministry work, he strives to provide both teaching and counseling for the people of God, through workshops and seminars through the church.

He has organized "The Institute For Higher Christian Consciousness," a 501(c)(3) nonprofit, to continue his work post-pastoring.

You can reach Rev. Polk at revwillispolk@gmail.com and through his website, www.TheIHCC.org

Chapter 10
Someone's Going to Eat Tonight
Candace Craw-Goldman

I looked at their faces. They were my community, my tribe . . . my family.

They would soon take my life.

They were gleeful upon approach, shouting, and grunting with pleasure. This was going to be easy. Holding their sharpened hunting sticks high above their heads, they began to point and jab them at me. They wanted me to throw myself off the cliff and save them the trouble of physical contact, but I stood my ground. They would have to pierce my flesh. They would have to force me. They would have to feel my skin break and have my blood on their sticks. I would be sovereign for my last breaths.

They pushed the little ones in front of them, encouraging them to participate. The last beats of my heart were excruciating, as I looked into the children's eyes. I felt anguish, not for myself, but for them. Life just didn't have to be this way.

I felt the air sweep my face as I fell. I smelled the sweet summer plant blooms, as my body knocked against the cliff face. I braced myself mentally for impact at the bottom but was surprised . . . none came.

Everything was more difficult living alone, but hunting was the hardest thing of all. I only had one set of eyes. Hunting was ever dangerous; hunting by myself, I felt terrifyingly vulnerable.

I had been tracking one of the small-hoofed deer, hoping for an easy kill. I hadn't eaten in multiple days and was weak and light-headed, but I was moving as quickly and quietly as I could, because if some-one, or something else might also be hungry, failure might be the end of me.

The little deer must have been quite young by the size of the print. I had been up this path so many times, I knew every inch of it. Every rock, every plant, every twist and turn. The little deer was moving up a narrow trail, and there was no other way down. I might be eating tonight.

But then, I heard noise behind me, and my blood ran cold. If it was a predator, I was now the prey. Slowly, I turned, and although they were fairly far off, I saw familiar faces. There was maybe a dozen of them, some mere children. One or two of them were family, and they, too, carried sharpened stick spears, used for hunting. But they were not quiet. They were grunting and laughing. They were not hunting for game. They were hunting *me*. My own odds just ran out.

I would soon die.

They hated me. No, they actually loathed me, because I was differ-ent. I had red hair, rather than the more common dull brown. They shamed me for having new ideas about making tools and suggesting more cooperative approaches to hunting. They laughed at my small size. They saw me as damaged and evil. They banished me. I'd survived for a number of weeks on my own, but since I hadn't died as expected, here they came to finish me off.

Instinct drove me continually up, but I was trapped, as doomed as the little deer. They knew it, and I knew it. Two more blind turns before the ground would give way to a sheer cliff on both sides. I saw the tail of the little deer, turning into the last few feet of the narrow trail. That is when I stopped and faced them, standing strong for as long as I could.

And then, fell.

I never felt the impact of the canyon floor. Rather, I found myself back up on the steep trail, feeling as if I were standing next to my tribe looking down but no longer in physical form. Their grunts continued. They lifted up the children in celebration, as they peered at the still, broken, and bleeding, red-haired body below . . . .

It was then that Dolores Cannon, my teacher, asked me what I thought about the scene. "Well," I said, considering the flesh of my form below, "*Someone* is going to eat tonight!"

In the background of the hotel ballroom, I heard the observers of my session, the others in Dolores' past life regression class, laugh nervously. The year was 2008, and I was her chosen demonstration subject. I was laying on a rollaway cot, deep in trance.

Dolores then asked, "How do you feel about what they did to you?"

I felt she was expecting me to say that I was angry, but I wasn't angry. I was sad. I had *experienced* the heart of that caveman in my own heart. I grieved the brutal ways of the tribe and their teaching of their young to continue the same cruel mob mentality. Their inability to consider new concepts evoked a deep, aching sadness for what could have been.

I learned many things about myself during that regression with Dolores. I am still, to this day, marveling at the relevance of my caveman existence. Its theme continues to present in my life and indeed, the world, as well.

Even more, discovering, then experiencing, this basic concept of consciousness exploration, I felt like I had been handed the golden key to explore absolutely anything and everything.

Perhaps the biggest revelation from my Higher Self during that regression was how this greater aspect of my consciousness is—has always been—communicating with me in a variety of ways. I could gain new understanding on all kinds of personal events, see them from a new perspective. Rather than simply wonder why something occurred, I could consider what message my Higher Self was attempting to convey in that experience.

Random events in my life weren't really random at all. Everything had meaning. Everything, like the time when I died at eleven years old . . . or at least when I thought I did.

It wasn't an accident or a huge trauma, pretty much just a regular day. Except for one thing: I had a fever.

We, my mom, dad, and little brother Randy, who was nine, lived in Tampa, Florida, in a tri-level house. The bedrooms were on the upper level, and my room was like an oven, with its obnoxiously bright, hot-red, shag carpet. Mom set me up in the much cooler den on the lowest level. I was bored and waiting for Randy to come home. It was a big day for him, as his class had been holding a major spelling bee, which he was determined to win. Finally, I heard the front door slam. I wanted to know what happened in the spelling bee! I heard footsteps overhead; Mom and Randy were going upstairs. Darn.

My curiosity was overwhelming. I decided go find out what happened. I stood up, and didn't feel too bad, so I headed for the first staircase. Suddenly, I was feeling so much better! As I headed up the main staircase, it felt as if my fever was gone. I felt fantastic and made my way to my brother's room. He was sitting on his bed, excitedly telling Mom how he had won the spelling bee.

"Look Mom, look what I won!" Randy unzipped his book-bag and out came the biggest Hershey's chocolate bar I had ever seen, all tied up in blue and silver ribbons. I started to say something just then, but my voice didn't work. Then I noticed my perspective . . . I was too high in the room. Confused, I felt my head bump ever so softly on the ceiling, like a helium balloon gently rising to touch a solid surface.

Panic set in. Human bodies don't float! I must be *dead*! In that instant, much like the snapping back of a rubber band, I found myself back in the den, inside my hot, heavy, fevered body. I hadn't gotten out of bed at all; I only *thought* that I did! Minutes later, Mom and Randy walked into the den. Randy held his huge Hershey bar over his head, as the blue and silver ribbons streamed down around his smiling face. Exactly the thing I saw him hold when I was upstairs *on the ceiling.*

I may have only been eleven, but I came to a simple and obvious conclusion. The person I knew as "me" was *not* inextricably connected to my physical body! Somehow, I left that body, and yet, I still felt like myself. I traveled to another location, and watched what was happening, and heard people talking. Everything I believed about life and reality changed that day.

My Higher Self's message was pretty clear, but I didn't have much context or anyone to talk to about it.

The one thing that I knew for certain was that, if I shared this experience with my mother, she would have kindly explained it away. Just as she explained away my prophetic dreams and other paranormal events that I'd shared. She was no different than any other adult in that regard, so I resolved to keep those kinds of things to myself. That resolution lasted long into adulthood.

In my early twenties and newly married, I had a series of powerful, unintentional, out-of-body experiences (OBEs). They were so strong and so uncontrollable to me, that I remember almost dreading closing my eyes. While the OBE of my childhood absolutely provided some comfort, these were different. I wasn't slipping easily out of my physical form. Rather, each event began with violent, overpowering vibrations and an overwhelming roaring noise. Instinctually, I fought against this energy out of fear.

I lost a lot of sleep and for a while, thought I might be going a bit mad. While this was happening, I was working towards my Bachelor of Fine Arts degree. One day it occurred to me that I could try to do some research. Surely others had experienced this kind of thing before. It was the early 1980's, pre-internet, so my only resource was using the card catalog at the school library. Thankfully, I found a book title that seemed like it might help. I have this vivid memory of pulling down the book, *Journeys Out of Body,* by Robert Monroe, from an upper shelf. Sitting right on the library floor, I began reading.

To say Robert Monroe saved my life might seem extreme, but it truly felt that way. More accurately, my Higher Self guided me to him to broaden my understanding of other kinds of realities available . . . realities like my childhood fever experience had proven, that we're not dependent on human form. I inhaled Monroe's words like a medicine, realizing my OBEs were a gift I could control. His writings continue to inform the way I see the world. If he is unfamiliar, look him up. Monroe actually invented a new word that is used by many awakened people today: *loosh*. It's a word that refers to a type of energy. It is a rabbit hole of a concept that can explain much of what has happened to humans throughout time and what is happening in our world today.

This metaphysical world-view was new. Brought up in a basic Christian tradition, I visited various churches with friends or extended family and attended summertime "vacation" Bible school with other young children. I sometimes asked uncomfortable questions to the adults in charge. Their responses were nonsensical, often robotic, and did not ring true, which confused me. If the grown-ups didn't know, or couldn't adequately, convincingly explain the origins of life and the purpose of humans and what happened exactly after we died, who in the world could?

As the years passed, I was exposed to other belief systems through travel and study, much of it variations on the Christian-based themes I learned in kindergarten. All the while, I collected more paranormal experiences, including prophetic dreams, visitations, powerful psychic messages, and spontaneous past life memories that I had once considered special daydreams created by a lively imagination. In fact, if I mentioned them, I was told "Oh, that's just your imagination."

In 1989, my brother Randy was killed, suddenly, by a reckless teenage driver. It was another huge awakening event. The trauma absolutely played its part, but I see, now, how Randy's Higher Self and my own Higher Self knew exactly what was coming. We were given profound last-minute gifts and many powerful clues. None of the clues were obvious or straightforward at the time, but in retrospect they were a blessing.

In the weeks leading up to Randy's death, we took a final trip together, skiing in New Mexico for a weekend. Our topics of conversation were extraordinary, the ideas of a young and newly awakened man. But barely 'awake' at the time myself, I had no real context for what Randy shared. He talked about "fake reality" systems, "games" humanity played, how important it was to help everyone around us, how he would be sure to help me when our parents were elderly. He introduced me to the concept of synchronicities, in particular the 11:11 on a digital clock, something I had never noticed myself. I have come to understand that synchronicities, and especially time prompts, are like winks or confirmations from the universe. For a long time, I thought 11:11 was simply Randy saying "hello."

Exactly one week before he died, Randy and his fiancé were dressing up to go to a formal dance. Randy became agitated and distraught, certain something terrible and horrible had happened to me. These were in the days before mobile phones. I was completely fine, just unreachable. Randy took Gina, his fiancé, home and then drove around town in tears, looking for me, to no avail. They never made it to the dance.

"I am just fine!" I told Randy when we reconnected the next morning —a statement that held true until one week later, when we received news of his death.

The weeks and months following Randy's death were filled with paranormal activity: physical manifestations, overwhelming dreams, and after-death communication directly from my brother. I felt like I was in a completely different world. My awakening had moved to a whole new level.

We are guided to our own expansion in so many ways. Dreams, meditation, paranormal experiences, hypnosis or quantum healing sessions, and even—sometimes especially—when we experience trauma, illness, or grief. Every choice we make, large or small, alters our course through the world our soul has set up for us to navigate. Even "accidents" are no accident.

Neither the caveman nor Randy experienced any real pain or trauma during their bodily deaths. Randy showed me exactly how and when he left his physical form, about thirty seconds before the truck hit him. Just like I, the caveman, went off the cliff, but never 'felt' the impact of the ground, Randy was already gone by the time the crash took place.

The boy who lost control of his truck and killed my brother had a life contract with Randy, and by extension, me and my family, as well. The caveman leader and the caveman I was, had other chances to work out their lessons. Of this, I am absolutely certain, because a part of me is still connected to that life and to that leader, too.

Information comes wrapped in big life events, but it is also delivered in even the smallest of ways. A stubbed toe, a flat tire, the sting of a wasp. The direction of the wind, the time you note on the clock, the color of the t-shirt you notice in your drawer and choose to wear that day. The shape of a cloud, the flower you see broken in the garden, the song playing on the radio as you head to a long-awaited appointment. All these things play a part in the 'timing' of your life and the messages sent and received.

We can all reconsider the events, relationships, and stories of our lives, both large and small, whether positive or negative. Any accident, every coincidence, and each situation we face can be gleaned for deeper meaning, to assist in continued growth and understanding of our ultimate path and purpose for life.

I am convinced that we live in a time where more humans than ever, all over the planet, are awakening to a collective potential so great, it might actually lead to a leap of indescribable consciousness evolution for humanity itself. The very fact that a book such as the one you hold in your hand exists, at this moment in time, is undeniable proof.

Candace Craw-Goldman is a wife, mother and grandmama, who wanted nothing more than to paint, live on a farm, and ride horses every day. A mysterious years-long chronic pain condition inspired her to explore alternative healing modalities with minimal results, until a supernatural experience directed her to Dolores Cannon, and the pain disappeared. Eager to help others, she began her life as a Quantum Healer and soon began working with Dolores, officially supporting Dolores' students and assisting in live classes and program creation. Candace worked with Dolores until her passing in 2014.

QuantumHealers.com got its start in 2008, supporting the practitioners Dolores trained. Today, it represents thousands of alternative healers of all modalities with its thriving community, worldwide directory, and education programs.

In 2017 Candace developed Beyond Quantum Healing—a heart-centered, freedom-based approach to consciousness exploration. Thousands of students around the world now practice BQH. The online course is available in five languages.

In 2023 Candace created Quantum Connect. QC is a fun, fast, no-trance method that helps clients experience how they are always connected to their Higher Selves. Quantum Connect is perfect for healers, counselors, coaches and anyone who is in service-to-others.

Candace received her Bachelor of Fine Arts and Master of Fine Arts in Painting and spent twenty-two years as a professional photographer, specializing in equine and rodeo imagery. She lives on a sprawling Kansas farm with her husband, horses, a mini donkey named Elvis, and assorted critters. Since 2008, she has volunteered regularly for 'Now I Lay Me Down to Sleep,' which provides remembrance photography for parents experiencing the death of a baby.

In addition to facilitating quantum healing sessions with clients around the world, Candace is also a pilot, author, speaker, gardener, snake wrangler, baby-animal rescuer, chicken egg collector, and energy portal docent.

She definitely, absolutely, will pick up her paintbrushes again very soon.

Candace's personal website https://candacecrawgoldman.com/

QuantumHealers.com Directory, Community, Support Forum and Classes https://quantumhealers.com/

Chapter 11
The Gift of the Equid
Kate Coldren

On April Fool's Day, 2023, working as a new barefoot hoof trimming professional, I was on my eleventh four-footed equid, trimming a skittish donkey, alongside her owner. Bending over her left hind foot, the donkey kicked me square in the face. I spun away from the impact, clutching my face. My nose and lip were bleeding, my ego bruised.

After waiting two days to be seen by a doctor, I finally called urgent care. A deep commanding voice on the other end of the line said they wouldn't see me; they feared that the optical nerve could get trapped in the fracture if my cheek bone had been broken by the impact. It was possible I could lose the mobility of my eye. I reluctantly agreed to follow instructions and get imaging. *Awesome start to the week*, I thought to myself, as I sulked my way to the emergency room.

The damage was, as I suspected, not as bad as it could have been, but I did have a broken nose on the right side of my face. Swollen and embarrassed, I called my manager and let him know I would be out of commission for a couple of days. My nine-to-five sales job does not require me to regularly dodge flying hooves.

A year prior, I had become a certified hoof trimming professional . . . one that doesn't use metal or nails. The flow state I entered while caring for hooves was magical. The equids are generally so grateful for humans who can make them feel good in their bodies, and being a flight animal, their feet mean the world to them. In some cases, it can mean the difference between life and death. However, there is another level to this non-verbal exchange between human and equid. Ray Hunt summarizes it well by saying, "The horse knows. He knows if you know. He also knows if you don't know."

This is true at the surface, but it is also true at a much deeper level. Horses have the ability to *feel into* human beings, gauging their level of authenticity and congruence. Horses get to places in a human being that another human just cannot access. There is a conversation happening between species, an interspecies exchange, which transcends the human mind. Humans can get caught up in the mind, forgetting our bodies, so these types of interspecies conversations bring us right back to nature, helping us remember that we, too, are born into this earth plane, just as any other mammal on this planet.

This wasn't the first time the universe had tried to get my attention. The previous October, a tree fell in front of my car on my way home from trimming some Arabians for a client. I had to backtrack and detour. When I got home, I was a bit shaken by the experience, while sharing it with my husband. But on reflection, I realized that the messages tend to get stronger when I wander from my path.

This time, "the accident" was a reminder to stop hyper-focusing on hooves. It is not just the feet! The more you work with the architecture and functionality of the hoof, the more the horse guides you to what they need.

It had been eight days since the incident. The pressure in my face was unbearable. I was certain something had been missed on the CT scan, but it was late Sunday night, and I had no desire to spend all night at the hospital. I went back to the hospital first thing Monday morning. Another scan sent me to an Ear, Nose, and Throat specialist to address the abscess that had developed in my cheek. As a former veterinary technician, I knew that, once this was lanced, I would feel better quickly. This was the consolation prize for nine years of service, caring for small animals. It was also the reason I sat at the dining room table, rinsing the pocket in my face with saline. I was probably the only person in the world torturing myself with this type of treatment.

A couple of months passed, and the story of this incident emerged again during my dental cleaning visit. I was due for my full mouth radiographs—at that moment, I realized exactly how lucky I had been. There were so many critical structures that could have been damaged by this event, but the dentist couldn't even tell the impact had occurred! I was hit in the "perfect" location; my jaw and teeth were alright, as was my occipital bone. Rather than calling it an accident, it was a warning for me to pay attention.

I later learned that the previous farrier had been fired for kicking the donkey. I was just the unfortunate individual that received the reciprocal blow. You see, energy cannot be created or destroyed. This energy—the energy of the trauma the donkey had suffered—lay dormant in her fascia . . . that is, until I, unknowingly, unlocked the trauma, allowing the energy to escape and transmute into something else. *I had become an alchemist.*

Gratitude for good health filled my form, and I recalled how I moved with the energy field around me. For a moment, I felt like Neo in *The Matrix*, feeling into the past, present, and future all at once. It was as if linear time was only a construct, and everything existed all at once.

* * *

As my path developed, I began to work with equids in new ways. I attended clinics, integrating the methodology of multiple equine clinicians. I spent time with the anatomy of the equine body. Through thoughts and words, I asked questions of the equids. Their voices began to get louder, as they realized their opinions about their bodies and their husbandry were being considered. This communication was not always easy—their answers were, often, painful to hear; sometimes, I would even feel their pain in my *own* body.

I recall three consecutive months where this process continued to build, the culmination of which was a Nahshon Cook Horsemanship clinic that I attended with two of my horses . . . each was to have a lesson. Nahshon helps his students reconnect with their horse through intuition, by quieting the mind and feeling into the body. The second day was a powerful experience, during which, I connected to my Higher Self and was reminded of my *soul agreement.*

Clifford, who was up first, is a warmblood, chestnut gelding, who came to me through a couple, who I would consider close friends. I had been present that day, five years earlier, when he was gifted to them, and I remember thinking that his eyes looked like they were bugging out of his head. His forehead was so broad and frog-like, that it made his eyes bulge, as if he had seen a poltergeist! At the time, I wanted nothing to do with him. Clifford then spent five years in a field with them. Thinking that I could assist him with some of the problems in his emotional and physical body, my friends passed him off to me. I took him in as a gesture of good faith, with the goal of bridging the gap between his soul and his physical form. I had a feeling he might be a great teacher.

We started the lesson with a discussion of tack—just the thought of a saddle and bridle made this horse tense up. I knew this because, as I considered bringing the equipment out to ride, Clifford's demeanor changed. He tensed his entire being, eyes glazed, shoulders frozen, hind legs braced deeply under his barrel. After processing the feedback from Clifford, we changed gears, and used movement to unwind his emotional ball of yarn, tangled by a series of humans doing the best they could with the tools they had. I find that humans and horse training leave imprints on horses unintentionally. If I can allow the horse to find the tail end and work through the web of knots, just maybe, peace can be uncovered or recovered.

Nahshon asked, "What would you like to do with this horse?" I wasn't sure yet, because I didn't know what discipline Clifford would really enjoy. It was a difficult question to answer, when I had gotten such a hard "no" from just thinking about the accessories of equestrian activities. This is where things got interesting and telepathic. I had started to get a little flustered and confused, myself, because there was so much energy being pointed our way from the auditing crowd of about thirty people on top of the dialogue between horse and instructor. I instinctually closed off. I put up a wall of energy to protect us both from the thoughts and judgments of those surrounding us. Beside me, Clifford began to yawn, a sign he had found peace in the quiet.

The following day, my horse of over twenty years, Max, took the stage. I put him on a lunge line, and he came out like the Hackney Horse[1] he is, at a huge powerful trot—the kind of entrance that would make anyone pause, catching their breath in their throat for a moment. Max and I share a long history, with many fascinating stories. He has been an outstanding teacher, while I have been a mediocre student, at best, for most of our time together. I have done many things wrong with this horse, one of which was to use draw reins[2] without understanding their biomechanical implications. For that reason, working with him brings back the haunting habits and insecurities of my younger Self; although, his patience has helped me grow over time. This lesson brought me back face to face with myself.

---

1. An elegant, high-stepping breed of carriage horse
2. Reins that are attached to a horse's saddle or girth and pass through the bit to the rider's hands; they provide added leverage for control

As a young person, I was much more confident once I was astride. I didn't handle horses much on the ground, because I hadn't done any groundwork growing up in New Hampshire. I just got on. So I did that here.

Throughout the lesson, Nahshon would ask, "Is this relevant to today's lesson?" From my perspective, the lesson was turning into a way to reconnect with my soul's purpose. Nashon gave quiet guidance to help Max lift his back and relax his neck forward and down towards his front feet. Nahshon spoke of "making the body parts hot and heavy," using this uncommon language to help change the energy of the body and sculpt it in rhythm and speed to slow down Max's steps. Nashon had a hypothesis that horses will *move into pressure* when they feel safe, like when you are holding hands with someone you love; therefore, by using the temperature gradient, it was possible to change the horses' posture. When a horse engages the correct muscles to carry a rider, their posture rounds and creates a bridge from back to front; that way, the rider can experience the brilliance of engagement and power that a horse can provide.

Where were we? It felt as if we were we traversing the deserts of Arrakis. The air was thick, but I didn't need to breathe. We were moving like a wave, our feet not touching the ground. Were we still on Earth? Maybe, partially. "Make his tongue hot and heavy," Nashon said, reconnecting me to the present. "His tongue is getting tired from holding the bit."

I dismounted.

Internally, I feared I would do too much.

Humans do too much to horses.

They take too much.

I have taken too much.

I have been experimenting with taking less.

My sense of time had been lost during those moments together; we had entered a space where time did not exist. I lost all bearing, and there was still a quarter of an hour remaining for our session. Nahshon asked why I dismounted, suggesting that, in the future, I check in with him first, so we could stay in communication with one another. I agreed. I had never done this before in a lesson . . . at least not that I was aware of. I had never "gone away," or "lost time." I had also never had an instructor respond to me with such kindness and with a sincere interest in my motivation for my actions.

I was still struggling; my insides were swirling. I stood there, quietly, while my horse expressed all that I was feeling. His feet danced as if the ground was on fire. I walked to the corner and sat on a pedestal. I waited. I waited for my body and my horse's body to allow the essence, the energy, to travel back down into the third dimension . . . back into *this* reality. The audience struggled with the safety of sitting in a corner with a horse that was full of energy. True, this was not a traditionally safe way to behave around horses, but this was so much deeper than just a riding lesson.

I walked back to the center of the ring and broke down, sobbing. Ugly crying. Holding the lead rope in my left hand, I wept for the partner-ship Max and I had . . . for all its strengths and its weaknesses . . . for the trials and tribulations. Where each discipline we tried, just didn't feel quite right. We would fail, but we got up and kept working towards traditional equestrian goals. We stayed the course—just being together was enough. I had spent many years, decades even, trying to figure out how to train this horse. Max reflected my own Self . . . my own journey . . . back to me, and it was hard to face. I was a human.

"Thank you for showing up," Nahshon said, over again, with the passion and sincerity of all of humanity behind him. Nahshon helped me find my way back into my body, bringing about a sense of peace. It was an epiphany! This was the first time I understood that, when I rode Max, I would "leave" my body. It was so seamless that it had never dawned on me before. But looking back, I recall, as a teenager, being offended by a friend and competitor who told me that I didn't listen to my coach when I rode. Perhaps it was because I wasn't fully in my body.

Many people, after my training sessions, wouldn't make eye contact with me. The vibration between these two horses and myself, and the changes we had made, was overwhelming for them. I could feel the commitment I had made, and the reminder was strong. But being vulnerable and crying like that in front of so many had created an uncomfortableness. As I walked around the venue, seeking connection from the auditors, I saw them turn away; the light that was exuding from me was overwhelming. It was a hard lesson—this is why we often hide our light from the world when our heart is not safe from judgment.

I stayed and watched the remainder of the lessons with other students. As the sun dropped low on the horizon, I loaded the two geldings for our ride home. I asked them, in my mind, to please help me get us all home safely. As we drove westbound on Interstate 40, I noticed a truck and trailer dragging a safety chain that was sparking on the pavement. With my mind, I gently pulled the chain to the right—divine timing popped the link free, and it moved off into the curb. Traffic slowed, and I felt a hoof paw the floor of the trailer . . . my navigation system had modified my route to take the next exit to avoid stopped traffic ahead. The horses were aiding our journey home.

The gravel crunched under the truck tires, as we rolled slowly into the single lane drive, bearing left under large oaks, and into the forest. I always roll my windows down to listen to which of my other horses will be the first to greet those that have traveled and are returning home. But tonight, under dark skies and starlight, there was only silence; the quiet of horses with sleepy eyes and shavings-covered bodies. The herd already felt the work that had unfolded like the first morning bloom.

The short days of December typically required many hours in head-lamps, doing routine chores. But the following evening was different; the high-frequency energy from the lessons remained, and under the winter constellations, I was reminded to say *yes* to the next step of the unfoldment. In the western night sky, as if in reply, there were silent red fireworks, a celebration for the unspoken agreement. From here, I trusted the synchronicity and the invitation to one of Earth's energetic vortexes, Bali, Indonesia.

The path of our lives is continuously unfolding in a beautiful balance of fate and free will. I find myself guided, in the transition of humanity, to the place where we can find peace in ourselves, reconnecting with nature, and modeling a new way of being in collaboration, rather than being dominated by competition and comparison. Keeping up with the Jones' will no longer serve the collective—through communion with horses, we can find strength in everyone's natural gifts.

There is a future where horses are humanity's teachers . . . where words become irrelevant, and we can feel what humanity desires to create. I envision a planet where we grow nutritious food, in proximity to where we sleep, rather than driving to the nearest fast-food joint. Where learning doesn't simply mean regurgitating answers for an exam but instead, actively feeds our soul. An existence in which we engage in meaningful activities . . . where we can spend our dollars repairing the earth, rather than depleting her. Priorities are changing as we awaken, and I am ready to observe the alchemy that will emerge from the gift of the equid.

Kate Coldren grew up in rural New Hampshire, where she fell in love with horses at age six. She began to take lessons twice a week, until her parents purchased her first horse when she turned thirteen. And she hasn't looked back since!

Kate competed at the Grand National / World stage in Oklahoma City, Oklahoma, with her Morgan horse, Fudge, in the thirteen and under English Pleasure division. In high school she worked at a small, private farm with six horses, Norwegian Fjords and Morgans, keeping them fit for carriage driving. This was also the time when Max, the Hackney Horse came into her life at age three.

Kate attended Randolph-Macon Woman's College, riding in their equestrian lesson program twice weekly, each semester, during all four years of university. She also played soccer all four seasons and swam competitively from sophomore to senior year. Kate was a graduate of the Susan B. Davenport Leadership Program, where, as a senior, she developed a Peace & Diplomacy residence community to help first-year college students with their transition. She was also an active member of the Randolph College Society of Physics Students, involved in planning and implementing the annual Science Day for local middle school students in the Lynchburg, Virginia area.

Kate blogged about her experience with the Retired Racehorse Project Thoroughbred Makeover with Horse Nation, in 2021, documenting her journey with New Prince, Luis, while training and competing in Competitive Trail and Freestyle disciplines.

Professionally, Kate spent nine years working in veterinary practices —from general practice to referral surgery—in numerous roles, including technician and surgical instrument specialist. In 2017, she transitioned to sales, supporting the veterinary industry for a manufacturing company. Most recently, she has transitioned to supporting the Anatomic Pathology laboratory by serving customers in North and South Carolina.

Reach out to Kate at resonance.equine.services@gmail.com

Chapter 12

We're Always in The Midst Of Awakening

Linda Alberga

Noticing my breath. Inhaling slowly and lengthening my exhales. Sitting up tall with a soft belly and observing the muscles in my face, the space between my eyebrows, and the tension in my jaw. Inviting you at this time, as you begin to read this chapter, to perhaps do the same. What does your breath cycle feel like right now? Is it shallow? Is it the first time you've noticed it today? Can you invite more length as you welcome your breath into your body? How does it feel to exhale with intention now that you've brought your attention here? Awareness of your breath, the one that *gives us life*, holds much beauty in that it brings you into the present moment. This gift, the one we cannot live without, has been rhythmically occurring, without thought, since the instance we came into this world. And it is one that, should you orient yourself with it daily and purposefully, will absolutely change your life—as it did mine just a few years ago.

I am the youngest of four children; born and raised in Montreal, Canada. My papa immigrated from Italy at eleven years old, and my mama grew up here, raised by parents who also immigrated from Italy. For as long as I can remember, I have been addressed lovingly as the baby of the family, the youngest of my widespread, big Italian family filled with many Zias, Zios, and cuginis (aunts, uncles, and cousins). I bring this up because, aside from deeply loving each one of my family members dearly, the energy and story around being the baby had shaped a considerable aspect of who I was when I was growing up. I mean, we've all heard these sayings, right? The oldest child is often seen as the most mature and responsible; there exists an unspoken expectancy to set the example for their siblings. The middle child has the "middle child syndrome" and can sometimes feel overlooked or unnoticed, while the youngest is typically perceived as the spoiled one who gets whatever they want. *What interesting stories and beliefs we've created and placed into the world as an unconscious way of expression.*

Notice, by the way, how I said that this is an *unconscious* story/belief cemented through words and verbalized as expressions that we throw around. What I mean by that is, we often don't realize the gravity of these expressions and the impact they have on each individual, especially when we are little humans. The beauty in this, however, was that it became a learning opportunity for me as I got older. Thankfully, it was always said playfully, and I was raised in a household where, above all, there was love.

My papa was (and still is) a hardworking man ensuring he always put food on the table and is the reason why my childhood was filled with my greatest memories. I partook in so many activities and was acquainted from the early age of three years old with my greatest passion: dance. My mama always said that as soon as I started walking, any time we went to family gatherings, there I was dancing away! Little did I know that, very early on, this was my soul's way of expressing itself, leading me to much of what I do today that is in alignment with my soul purpose.

They say humans are often influenced by their environments. That could be through family, socially, culturally, or even the physical spaces they inhabit. I was brought up with the mindset that I would go to school, make my way through university, find my mate, get married, and start a family. The many TV shows and movies I watched echoed similar messages, reinforcing those ideas and stories, creating the narrative in my mind, as to what life 'should' and 'will' look like.

These unconscious subscriptions, which occurred unknowingly as part of how the brain and mind develop in humans, became the beliefs and programming that ultimately contrasted with my reality, subsequently placing me on my path to self-discovery.

When I was in high school, academics were not my strength; however, I headed to college anyway, because it was what you do after high school. Soon, I found myself feeling drawn to the hotel industry—I loved to work with people, and it very much conformed to the idea of getting a job to make money. So I left college and went to work. Interestingly enough, without consciously knowing it at the time, life was already revealing its magic, demonstrating how it continually guides you towards your path of highest expression, especially when you are off course.

I very much enjoyed what I did, but for a variety of reasons, things started to shift at work . . . the environment started to become toxic. Even so, the thought of quitting meant I would have to tell my parents, who would worry about me; plus, who likes change? It's scary and feels incredibly uncomfortable. At least that's how I *used* to view change, mostly because I didn't know better. Come to think of it, that exact thought pattern was another one I adopted from my surroundings.

Today, looking back to this time that was occurring in my twenties, I realized I was already setting out on my own unique journey. I mean, I wasn't even up to par with all of the other imposed timelines suggested by society and my family. I was far from being at the height of my career and wasn't even close to marriage or babies. As my external experiences differed from the invisible expectations cast by the conditioning I'd been subjected to, physical responses within my body began to occur. While enduring the ongoing discomfort in my workplace, I began to experience anxiety, something I've never endured before, and it became unbearable.

It took months, as I would grapple with the fear of leaving, when finally, a beautiful and trusted doctor who cared and looked out for my well-being, wrote a letter to my employer's human resources department, stating I would no longer be returning to my job. This earth angel is one of many I've encountered in this lifetime. In hindsight, recalling this part of my journey validates how *we are always in the midst of awakening* and will connect with humans along the way that are guiding us to our true essence. As I reflect on these occurrences, I recognize that those moments that didn't align with societal expectations of career timelines or that urged me to tolerate a toxic work environment were all, in fact, my guiding lights to finding *myself*—my unique Self—and understanding *who I am*. This is when I came to realize that I need to hold in high regard *what brings me happiness* when it comes to work, which led me to finding my true purpose.

From this point forward, I decided it was important to follow what made me happy. I got involved with personal training, something I had always been interested in. This felt like a dream because, here I was, doing something I wholeheartedly enjoyed and could see my future in. Once I submerged myself in this field, change didn't feel so scary anymore. I was receiving different opportunities, expanding my knowledge and proficiency, eventually aligning within an environment that introduced me to more than just personal training.

At this stage, I also overcame the very traditional suggestion, as the baby of the family, to stay home with my parents until I got married. My life took yet another major shift once I came into my own living space. When I settled into my new home, living on my own and being in my own energy felt incredibly different. Without a second thought, I decided that I didn't want to have a TV in my place, which unintentionally freed up more time for self-exploration. I was working quite a bit, and any time I did have to myself, I spent on cooking fresh meals, moving my body, journaling, and tuning into podcast episodes that piqued my curiosity. I had also been introduced to breath practices during this phase of my life and *that* was the gateway to unlocking parts of my being I didn't even know existed.

Though meditation was initially foreign to me, gradually incorporating practices like consistent breath work and stillness attuned me to the power of my thoughts. This is what validated my decision to only listening (and consuming) things I *chose* to listen to. Coaches I was surrounded by reiterated that what we consume—in all facets—becomes a part of who we are and thus, who we become. I learned that taking responsibility (re·spon·si·bil·i·ty - *the* **ability** *to* **respond**), had a lot to do with my day-to-day choices and that I had the potential to design my life. This empowering enlightenment, that humans are creators and that we are meant to create our reality, came from authors like Don Miguel Ruiz, Paulo Coehlo, and Esther Hicks. Deepak Chopra was also one to shed light on the understanding that we are not our body, nor our mind. Suddenly, I was looking at life through a very different lens! It's as though I came across these humans, that I was divinely guided to, so that I could meet *my* true essence. Their teachings acclimatized me to aspects of my being that had lain dormant; yet once awoken, expanded my perspective on this human experience.

I would take time at home, my safe haven, to reflect on these new revelations through an expression I coined, *the power of the pen.* Upon rising, and again at night before bed, I would journal. This really started to deepen my connection within my own being and made me feel like I was actually speaking to that voice I have always been in exchange with, although unaware. This tangible action of writing down my thoughts, and seeing them in the physical form, made what was in my mind more real. This is where I learned that our thoughts become our actions and behaviors, which eventually creates our reality. Journaling really brought me closer to my true Self. There was no room for overthinking. The pen would just move, and I was willing to write how I felt about these newfound perspectives and what was *really* going on in my life—good, bad, happy, sad . . . my desires and aversions. I held myself in a space to get really honest, deciphering considerations by asking meaningful questions such as: What was important to me? How did I want to experience life? What makes me happy? What makes me feel good? What speaks to my heart? How do I want to experience love? How do I want my friendships to look? What did it mean to be surrounded by humans I felt aligned with?

These inquiries unveiled pieces of me that brought me closer to my authenticity. There was so much beauty in taking the time to get to know myself, as it guided me to the practice of Self love. Can you really call in community or even a partnership that aligns with your deepest desires and dreams if you don't fully know yourself or *love yourself*?

The concept that everything begins with "I" was seeded by a holistic health therapist named Paul Chek, whose podcast I came across around this time. I was fascinated by his work, and I knew something was drawing me to his teachings—any time I would listen to his episodes, it felt like lightbulbs were turning on in my mind and throughout my body. Within a couple of years, after the whispers within grew to *insistent* calls, I applied to the Chek Institute to become a holistic health practitioner myself. The journey I've been on ever since has served the evolution of my continued personal development, along with what I now understand as my purpose and soul mission—to be of service to fellow humans in the name of health and wellness. Voilà (as they say in French): the power of reflection!

This path of self-discovery magnetized other humans onto my path, uncovering pieces of my soul that were yearning to be explored. The wisdom of my body kept directing me to facilitators that are still current mentors in my life. My Reiki Master opened me to the world of energy medicine and enhanced my connection to my Higher Self and the unseen world. My willingness to be open and learn brought me to a deeper sense that we are all connected to a greater whole. Sessions with my Reiki Master heightened my self-awareness and strengthened my innate wisdom to heal, by forging closer connections to those that came before me.

When I learned that my soul has come here to be the change in my lineage and stop generational trauma from continuing, the subscriptions I once acceded to were now being dismantled. I vowed to do this inner work to live the life my soul came here to experience but also to honor my ancestors who are the reason why I have the liberty to create my human experience. Since I've detached from the stories I was carrying that didn't belong to me and come into a space where I now co-create with the universe, life has become everything I've dreamed of and more!

Accepting that our human experience is not meant to be linear, I've integrated a more conscious way of living by navigating the inevitable ebbs and flows with the tools and practices I have acquired along the way. Learning how to regulate my nervous system has been transformative. Shifting from living in a constant sympathetic state (fight, flight, or freeze), which I existed in for the majority of my life, to a parasympathetic state has supported me in so many ways—my digestion, inflammation in the body, my relationships, and how I create my dream-affirming life. Embodying this awareness enhanced my capacity to curate more balance. It's what shifted me from being a *reactive* human to a *responsive* human. Teachers I admire taught me the importance of spending time in nature as *we are* nature. We live in a time where it is so easy to lose track of the days, because we are often *inside and doing*, instead of *outside and being*. Since I began spending more time outdoors in stillness and in quiet, I've felt much more creative and inspired to bring to fruition what my *mind's eye* sees.

I've also intuitively come into balance with my cycle, emphasizing the notion of deep congruence with my mind, body and spirit (which could be a whole chapter or even a book in itself). Practices led by an astrologer I followed online guided me to harness the ever-present energy of the cosmos, which is an integral part of who we are. Working with the moon cycles to clear and let go of what is not serving me and setting intentions to take inspired and aligned action during certain times of the month founded coherence that tapped me into the mysticism of this experience.

In a world where life is constantly busy and there are *a lot* of distractions and noise, it is imperative to know that the power is within us. We choose. We create. The louder your inner voice is, the further you are from your divine path. The more aligned you are, the call to get even more still is asked of you. Pain is here to teach us. Lean into resistance, while remembering that we don't always have to learn by going against the grain. We are in Earth school. Nothing is permanent. We can change our narrative. What *feels* good, follow it. What doesn't, ask why and take notes—either stay and learn, or let it go.

Embrace the journey as it unfolds. The destination will continue to shift. Falling in love with the process will give you more ease. Follow your heart, as it will never lead you astray. Practice gratitude; what you appreciate, appreciates. Words are powerful. Synchronicities are here to show you the unseen magic. Trust. Believe. Know that what you desire, desires you. What you see in your mind's eye is available to you. Let your vessel guide you. Take inventory of what's going on in your mind, as everything derives from thought. Breathe intentionally. Drink clean water. Nourish your body with food that's alive. Move your body. Take care of your sleep. Identify core values. Lead with love.

Life is a *journey*. Nature doesn't happen overnight; that's why there are seasons.

Cultivate chi. Get outside, feet on the earth. Listen with your heart. Learn. Integrate. Apply. Embody. Share your gifts. Be yourself. Play more. Have FUN! And remember, we are social creatures that are meant to connect with other humans, as they are potent mirrors and reflections for us to understand ourselves more deeply. Align with mentors, teachers, and like-hearted humans, for community enriches your life and is your birthright to experience joy, connection and growth.

Linda Alberga is a certified Holistic Health Practitioner and Energy Medicine Woman who facilitates journeys into self-discovery and exploration. It is with deep integrity and her own continued integration of learnings that she shares with others the potency of continually coming back to Self. Imparting the significance of self-awareness and inner awakening, Linda teaches the magnitude of proactively participating in the pursuit of honoring your body, mind, and spirit.

Through postural evaluations supporting spinal alignment and physical imbalances, physiological assessments, nutritional guidance, introspective practices, and the Japanese modality Reiki, Linda guides those she supports by connecting them with their inner compass. She acquaints fellow humans to the wisdom of their bodies with the understanding that all we experience *without* comes from within. She teaches the power of present-moment awareness, while sharing practices around building a deep sense of intuition, guiding one through the exploration and understanding of their subconscious mind and belief systems. Her group experiences entail similar themes and hone the power of community.

With great intention and purposeful guidance, Linda's support unlocks one's innate gifts, leading them to live their highest expression. Supporting their coherence to the interconnectedness of our multidimensional selves, her guidance leads individuals to living their soul's purpose in happiness and in health.

To delve deeper into holistic well-being with Linda, tune into her *Ordinary People* podcast on Spotify & Apple.

For daily inspiration and insights, follow her on Instagram: @lindaalberga

To learn more about Linda's work and explore opportunities for collaboration, visit: www.lindaalberga.com

Chapter 13
Transforming Trauma into Healing
Penni Vachon, DNP

I grew up Catholic and left the church in my teen years. I always struggled with the belief that I had to confess my sins to another human sitting in a wooden box and ask his permission for repentance. Thankfully, my father was Lutheran and supported me leaving the Catholic church. He encouraged me to explore several religions before I found my community. Although, I can thank those nuns in my early years for making me ambidextrous, as being left-handed just wasn't allowed. I always felt more spiritual than I did religious.

I had a trauma filled childhood, including sexual trauma from a very young age, that persisted into my tween years. I had to grow up quickly; I became the caretaker for my grandfather (also my molester) by the age of ten, which required me to learn how to carb count and dose insulin for him. I was also forced to pretend to be my missing cousin (presumed kidnapped when I was three) to comfort my grandfather while he lay on his deathbed.

Unfortunately, my family was riddled with ancestral trauma. Generations of sexual abuse, alcoholism, and drug addiction plagued my extended family. I found solace in my books and my education throughout my childhood.

I chose to forego the traditional party life of high school and instead, focused on ensuring that my friends were safe and well tended to. I was the self-proclaimed designated driver for the parties, as I couldn't bare the thought of something happening to one of them that I could have prevented. I would drop them off at the parties and then go to the library, only to return a few hours later to drive everyone home. I focused on school—my goal was to become a surgeon and travel to work with the world's most impoverished people.

I used those traumas and life circumstances to become stronger and more resilient. I learned, early, that I could only rely on myself. Still, my initial high school years were plagued with severe bullying and an eating disorder.

Thankfully, the universe brought my husband, Kevin, into my life when I was seventeen. I have always said he was my reward for having such a traumatic childhood. We got married when I was eighteen; I had my first daughter at age twenty-one. By twenty-four I was a full-time mom to my three beautiful daughters. I started nursing school a few weeks before my twenty-fifth birthday, while my youngest was only six months old and exclusively breastfeeding. Again, my darling husband went out of his way to drive the girls to my campus so I could breastfeed her every two hours until she turned one.

My "journey" officially began on January 25, 2019. I was gifted my first Reiki session and had no idea what I was about to get myself into! Going into that session, I had absolutely no idea what Reiki was, what medical intuition was, and even less knowledge about spirituality and all of the possibilities that would be coming my way.

I recall the session vividly. To say I was a skeptic would be an understatement. I texted my husband my last known address and said, "If you don't hear from me in two hours, assume I've been killed and call the police." I met with a very sweet woman who had no idea what we were about to encounter together or that she would become a pivotal part of my story.

After a brief discussion of how the session would work, I laid on the massage table and surrendered to the process. This was no small feat, as I am a self-proclaimed control freak. She started with a weighted eye mask and told me that I would hear her ring her Tibetan singing bowl three times to signal both the start and completion of our session. *I have no idea what that is, but I'm sure I'll figure it out*, was my last thought before being thrust into my first out-of-body experience.

With my heart pounding and my mind racing, I heard the third ring of the bowl and was immediately taken back to a memorable day in my childhood. I was watching a scene play out that I knew too well. Thirteen-year-old me sat on a large rock down at the river behind my house. I had my feet in the water as I had an out loud conversation about taking my own life. I was listening to myself reason that if I went through with it, then I would never be a surgeon, and I wouldn't be able to change people's lives. I also reasoned that if I *did* go through with it, then nobody would ever get to hurt me again, and I would finally be free.

As I watched this scene play out, I looked towards the hill that led down to the river from behind the church that was next door to my house, and I saw a pair of bare feet walking down the path towards me. I saw myself get up and walk down the riverbed, around the corner, and then back up onto the road. As soon as my feet hit the pavement of the road at the house next door, I was pulled back into my body. I looked to my left, and my Nana was sitting with me. She died on September 11, 2010. Surrounded by the most beautiful bright, white, light, Nana said, "I am so proud of you! You are helping so many people, and you are going to change so many lives. Just keep moving forward."

As she finished talking to me, the brightest light I had ever experienced seemed to move through my body, from my head down to my toes. The light was so bright I was squinting, yet I was also aware that I was wearing a weighted eye mask and that the light had to be coming from inside me and not from the room. As the light passed through me and left my feet, I heard the third ring of her bowl again, and I was fully awake. I lay there for a moment processing what had just happened.

I removed the mask, and my practitioner asked if I wanted to talk about the session. I replied, "Not really . . . I don't know what just happened." She asked if it would be alright to share her experience. "Yes," I answered. She sat down in the chair across from the massage table and proceeded to tell me that she saw me as a warrior. She went on to say that my guides gave her a message for me because they knew I wouldn't believe her. I lay there thinking to myself, *Who the Hell are these guides she's talking about?* The very clinical and analytical mind I have was trying so hard to process her statements.

She went on to say that she had never seen anything like what she just experienced with my guides. They were standing arm and arm, linked, protecting me. She explained that there were three of them—they were powerful and were always with me. My guides wanted me to trust my intuition more and accept that I am a medical intuitive. I confidently responded, "Yes, of course I am intuitive. I am a nurse, and I have nurses' intuition." Laughing, she replied, "Do you really think that is what you have?" "Yes! My nursing instructors told me that all nurses have a gut instinct that guides us," I retorted, slightly appalled.

Continuing with her debrief, my practitioner went on to tell me that my guides knew I would be in denial and gave her some information to help me see my gift. She said, "They are asking that you simply dip your foot into the pond of intuition and possibility . . . you don't have to jump fully in." Further, my guides told her to have me recall times over my career where I just *knew* something was going to happen or that something was wrong with someone without truly knowing how or why.

Perhaps most significantly, the guides shared a very specific incident that had occurred, in which a friend had been given some news about her father. I intuitively knew that he was dying of cancer, not battling pneumonia as she had been told, so I pressed her to fly home to see him. When she arrived, she was informed that her father had metastatic cancer. He went on to live for only a few short weeks. She would not have flown there if I had not pushed her, insisting that she go.

As the practitioner was relating this story—with eerie accuracy—my mind started to become overwhelmed. I believe she could sense that I was starting to shut down, so she, instead, offered me a couple of books to help me see the possibility of what she had shared. The first book she suggested I read was *Proof of Heaven* by Dr. Eben Alexander. The second book was *Awaken the Spirit Within* by Rebecca Rosen. I downloaded both books and dove headfirst into what eventually became my spiritual awakening.

During the journey into my awakening, I was blessed to have been exposed to a variety of modalities, including massage therapy, acupuncture, Reiki, hypnosis, tarot readings, shamanic healings, and so much more. I also had a few trusted friends that made up my "spiritual inner circle."

I relied on my father, in the early days, to help me fill in the parts of my childhood that my conscience had blocked out for obvious reasons. I also called upon him to help me figure out who I was meant to be. He shared an interesting story with me about a mediumship session he had experienced when I was only eight years old, in which he was told I was shrouded in a golden aura and would become the healer's healer. He said the news shook him so deeply that he gave up studying numerology and put away all of his spiritual explorations—that is, until I rekindled this in him through the questions I was asking.

I bought lots of books on medical intuition, spiritual awakening, and anything that I thought would add to my toolbox of knowledge. I followed social media accounts that I felt resonated with my search to help me figure out who I was meant to be.

Over the following few years, I had several opportunities to work with mediums, psychics, mystics, and trance channels. Each of those opportunities added to my toolbox. I had an interesting session in June, 2020, in particular, during which, I was told by a well-known mystic and prophet: "In October, your ego will be stripped, and you will no longer be able to hide your true Self." I saw this as a challenge and thus, shut down all of my meditation and spiritual practices by mid-September, in preparation for what I was hoping to avoid in October. I did the same thing in September, 2021 as well.

In September 2022, I gave myself the best birthday gift I could have —a trip to a Transpersonal and Trauma Healing Hypnosis (TTHH) weekend retreat. I released so much trauma in those two intense days of healing! I called Kevin on my four-hour drive home, explaining that I was different in all ways: spiritually, emotionally, mentally, and physically. I went on to tell him, "I am a badass, and I am fucking awesome!" Tearfully, my husband replied, "There she is! The woman I have loved for twenty-nine years. I have been waiting for you to see what I see."

A few weeks later, in the middle of October, 2022, I had my first earth medicine journey, during which, my ego was quickly dissolved, and I was allowed to truly envision myself as a healer. I immediately sat up from my journey with the realization that the prophet didn't mention WHICH October, but I was confident she meant this one! I turned to my friend and gasped, "Why did you let me do this in October? Now everyone is going to know who I really am!"

In November, 2022, I took my mother, daughter, granddaughter, and a small group of friends away for a weekend of immense healing in which we shared Reiki, energy healing, trauma releases, and earth medicine. A few weeks later, I gifted myself another TTHH weekend, except this one was focused on healing the healers. For me, the combination of trauma hypnotherapy, along with deeply profound earth medicine journeys, over a short period of time, was the catalyst I needed to help me release my ego and step onto my true path.

In hindsight, though, I would not have stacked the TTHH with earth medicine so closely together, as I found myself in a full spiritual crisis by January, 2023. Fortunately, I had heard many stories of people's spiritual awakenings over the past few years and was able to identify that my perceived existential crisis was actually my moment of awakening.

Unfortunately, this happened at approximately three in the morning.

I found myself in bed, recovering from a recent surgery, feeling and believing as though each breath was my last. I had a brief moment of awareness that, as I looked down at myself in bed, I had no body below the waist. I also had a moment of clarity in which I knew that I had a choice: wake up Kevin to take me to the emergency room and explain I was in the throws of a spiritual crisis or have him drive to my office and get me the supplies to give myself intravenous (IV) fluids to override the disconnect of body and soul. I opted for the latter. Kevin quickly rushed there and back home, and together, we started my IV line and had the fluids running. Over the following twelve hours, I gave myself a total of three liters of fluids, which finally allowed me to remain fully in-body.

I recall talking with a friend and spiritual mentor a few days later, describing my incident. She confirmed my suspicions were correct—

that I had, in fact, had an awakening. She went on to share that I fully activated my Kundalini energy and would be able to do so with much more ease in the future.

Today, I own a thriving integrative, primary care practice, where I am able to incorporate both my Eastern and Western modalities into caring for my patients. I am also a Reiki Master teacher and a certified Transpersonal and Trauma Healing Hypnotherapist. I host regular healing retreats, incorporating trauma hypnotherapy along with other modalities, such as craniosacral therapy, massage therapy, reflexology, somatic therapy, and shamanism.

I have a clarity that I did not have prior to 2019. I use my gifts as an intuitive healer for the good of the people and the planet. I am proud of myself for the journey I have made. The introvert in me definitely fought her way here, but I am eternally grateful for the process.

I am blessed to have been able to bring Reiki and energy healing to each of my daughters, my husband, and my mother, in addition to countless students over the years. I am also honored to have been trusted by so many people along the way to be a part of their healing journey, as well.

I often advise people to just stay open to the possibilities that come their way. I believe our strength comes from allowing ourselves to be vulnerable and open to receive. Too often, people have closed themselves off as a result of past trauma, so trusting themselves to be able to grow and heal is often a challenge.

I've also noticed that I have more patience today than I did prior to my awakening. I am able to be more authentic about my gifts. I proudly let my light shine bright, knowing that I will help many, but that, conversely, I may also be too much light for others. I don't allow the darkness of those wounded souls to deter me in any way.

Dr. Penni Vachon is an award-winning nurse practitioner, energy healer, and author. Penni married her high school sweetheart, Kevin, at age eighteen. Together, they have three daughters. One of her best accomplishments is her role as Gigi to her grandchildren.

Penni's traditional Christian upbringing led her down a path of deep investigation, which ultimately led to self-discovery through her spirituality. As a teenager, she began to question what she was told was the "religious norm," and this continued well into her adulthood.

This inquisitive approach to life led her to alternative medicine and integrative healing practices. Through this journey, she became a Reiki Master teacher and a certified Transpersonal and Trauma Healing Hypnotherapist. Penni is also a medical intuitive.

Penni's deep love for learning pushed her to earn both her Master of Science in Nursing and her Doctor of Nursing Practice at the University of Alabama at Birmingham. She opened her private practice, Lowcountry Wellness Center LLC, in Charleston, South Carolina, in August, 2017, as she was finishing her last semester of her doctoral program. She has won numerous awards from her community, including the Charleston's Choice Award for "Best Family Doctor" in 2019. She is considered an expert in her field of direct primary care. Penni is also a Lyme-literate nurse practitioner, as she personally battles the chronic illness herself.

Her desire to integrate spirituality with physical and emotional healing led her to create the PEACE Center for Healing LLC. The concept for the PEACE Center came to her during a meditation and is an acronym for personal, esoteric, ascending, consciousness, and evolution. She incorporates her spiritual practice into her everyday living.

To contact Penni visit: www.peacecenterforhealing.com

Chapter 14
I Have No Idea Where I Am
Priscilla Keresey

Rousing from sleep, abruptly or gradually, eventually achieves a point in a process when the act of waking is finished; you can say with conviction, "Yes, I'm awake." Others may observe us to be up and about, fully alert, but in truth the state is entirely subjective. Only I can say of myself, "I'm awake."

If only self-discovery were this definitive! No matter how many books or classes I learn from, understanding what it means to be *me*, alive, here and now, can only ever be a personal experience. Only I can describe where I am, how far I've come, or how it feels to be where I am. So if you were to ask how I got here, the first thing I'd say is, "Got where?"

This is my road to travel alone and therefore, rife with the perils of any journey: Am I lost? Are others farther ahead than I am? Did I make a wrong turn back there? And the most angst-ridden question of all: Am I on the right path to begin with? I've often wished for a guide on this road, someone who'd been here before, to help me out at a crossroads, to encourage me to keep going, or even to say, "Stop running so fast! Try to enjoy the journey, and worry less about the destination."

So let this caveat precede my story, because I don't *know* where I am or where I'm going, nor do I know how long I have to get "there." What I do know is that I'm not alone, and neither are you. Take inspiration from the stories you read, but don't take directions. Nobody else can tell you where you are or how far you've come. In Genesis 2:21, we read, "The Lord God caused a deep sleep to fall upon Adam, and he slept." Nowhere in that story is it written that Adam *wakes up*, so trust that you're in good company if you've felt befuddled or lost.

For me, awakening is a broadening of the *conscious perception* of myself. I am aware, finally, that the source of all Life, in which I live and move and have my being, is *me*. I am the painter and the painting; the writer and story. There is no separation between All That Is and who I Am. I recognize now that I am created by Life, as an expression of Life, and that *I am Life aware of itself* at the same time.

A memorable point in my awakening was grasping that I will never consciously comprehend Creation. My rational mind will never be able to quantify that I was created from Life, by Life, to live. Accepting this allows me to stop striving to live, and instead, simply, to be alive.

Because living is inseparable from creating, I also accept that because I'm living, I'm creating, and because life and creation are outside of time and location, there is never a beginning, midpoint, end, or absolute milestone along the way of either. You and I are a process, *in process*, eternally. So my advice to you, if you're still reading this is: take your time; stop trying to figure things out; allow yourself to be filled with wonder, even in the frustrating moments. If you're having trouble "letting go"—*add in*. Stop trying to correct what's wrong . . . we can't *not* experience, so if you unwittingly created an experience you don't like, instead of trying to *not* be impacted by it, try to add joy in. Life is additive, not subtractive. Get back on track by allowing grace to return, and grace will overwhelm the negative.

Before I reached this stage of waking up from the same sleep afflicting Adam, I was searching outside of myself for succor and grace. I spent a solid year appealing to God with only one prayer: *that the Holy Spirit come into my life.* I wanted so desperately to know that God loved me, because my experience with love made me doubt I knew what it was.

My solid Catholic upbringing was a lot more show than substance. I was privileged to be raised by educated, upper middle-class parents who made sure my siblings and I had everything a child would need to succeed—at least on paper. In practice, my mother was cold, unyielding, and critical. From her, I learned to doubt myself, question my worthiness, and confuse my feelings with hers. I can never remember a time when I felt secure in her love for me.

It's no surprise, then, that I developed all kinds of dysfunctional behaviors to manage my unconscious search for love, including an eating disorder. I'm grateful for bulimia, though, as it led me to two profound experiences.

The first was a sonogram of my heart. I don't know why, but as I watched the black-and-white image of my heart beating, I was overcome with pity. This mighty little organ worked so hard, while I actively worked against it, and I *felt* that heartbreak. Nature strove tirelessly towards its happy perpetuation despite all of my efforts to destroy it. I didn't stop purging, but I felt love that came from me, for me, and it was unlike any previous experience—I've never forgotten how moved I was for those few minutes.

The second was several years later when, still bulimic, I took the advice of a friend and went for a past life regression. I knew for the first time, then, that I had a spirit that existed eternally while my present woes came and went.

This was my first *intentional* metaphysical experience. I had expected to see myself as in a movie, full color, sound, and safely removed from any personal emotional response. Instead, I "awoke" in a much earlier century, aware that I was looking at my feet through my mind's eye. I was smack dab in the middle of a person, looking out from his eyes, at the ground around my feet, and then perceiving the people gathered around me. In that instant, I understood that I was living a religious vocation among other men in a small, silent community. My dominant emotion was joy, though the faces looking back at me projected only sorrow. I felt conviction, faith, and the kind of love that was just like the pity I felt for my heart.

This, I also knew—I was longing for God so deeply that I was readying to leave my community on the hill and head down to the valley, where I planned to lay down and die to be with Him. I would accomplish this by foregoing all food and water. When it left the body of that brother, my spirit knew immediately that I'd made a dreadful mistake. God had given my spirit the gift of a physical life and instead of enjoying it, I'd denied myself every expression of it. It was as if I'd been given a gorgeous coat but left it hanging in the closet because of the mistaken notion that God would want me to keep it pristine and not relish the use of it.

During the regression, the therapist had me consider changing the outcome. Instead of leaving the community where we lived so poorly, in silence, scraping out a meager living from a dry garden, waking in the cold night for prayers, castigating, denying, and belittling ourselves for being human . . . instead of leaving that physically impoverished life to die, I'd leave it to go down from the hill to the town below. There I'd eat, drink, dance, hear music, converse, argue, have sex, sleep deeply, work hard, earn money, and spend it. Imagine that!

When our session was complete, I walked home to my apartment in New York City, completely changed. I lingered outside restaurants, where I could smell delicious meals cooking; I walked through a grocery store, amazed at how serene I felt. I couldn't bear to be around food before this, and I continued testing myself all the way home. In that way, I proved to myself I was cured.

In pre-internet days, finding more information about metaphysical ideas meant looking at book and cassette tape catalogues, picking up newsletters from funky occult shops in the East Village, and going to the public library. It also meant keeping those ideas to myself—if you think New Age topics cause some eye-rolling these days, you wouldn't believe the mockery and ridicule in the early '90s, even in an "anything-goes" place like Manhattan.

I persisted, and in time, I became a hypnotist and regressionist myself. I attended countless seminars and listened to self-styled gurus. I studied crystals and herbal spells, I meditated, prayed, astral traveled, practiced out-of-body techniques, learned tarot, Reiki, and channeling. I picked up and discarded healing modalities and meta-physical ideas as though I were tasting every dish at an abundant buffet. I took in more of what I liked and left behind what didn't sit well with me. I grew; I know I did.

And yet . . . something was missing. Years of diving deeply into "spiri-tual" quests excited me and allowed me to expand my self-definition but left me searching still, and for what, I couldn't define. So now my search for love took on a different tone. I no longer wondered whether I deserved it; now, I wondered what it felt like. I had no other reference but that heart sonogram so many years ago—the emotion of which I could still feel, and therefore knew, having felt it once, that I hadn't felt it since.

By now, about fifteen years after my heart sonogram and ten years since my past life regression, I was well established as a professional hypnotist, psychic, and medium. I was more focused in my search for a connection to God. I was no longer consuming "anything and everything" New Age to deepen my spiritual experience. I'd grown a little jaded in the "spiritual" arena, having met teachers and read authors who declared themselves above others, anointed by God. I knew by then that Life and Creation weren't reserved only for *special* people. Grace was not dispensed by merit; this I knew to be true. We inherited Life and Love in amounts given equally to all. We didn't need to earn it, prove ourselves worthy, or only use it in the service of others. It was ours to use or abuse according to the degree of awareness in our creative abilities. I determined myself to be ready to serve God with what I'd already learned. No more studying for me, I was ready to take action. So for a year, I prayed daily and intensely, "Holy Spirit, come into me. Show me yourself." And I waited.

One thing I'd seen across each of my client bases was a stunning lack of self-esteem. All of us were searching for something outside of ourselves; I thought to myself, at times, that I needed a guru, a guide, *someone* to anoint me, declare me ready, "initiate" me, or award me permission to develop. I often wondered whether I needed to go on a spiritual journey to *find* myself. The problem, which I also saw in my clients, was that we were all looking in the wrong place: outside of ourselves.

In service to myself and these clients, I began to improve my own self-esteem. It was then that I first collapsed the separation I'd perceived between me and God. I was reading *Science of Mind,* by Ernest Holmes, other New Thought authors, and Gnostics. I applied New Thought principles to my life and tracked unimaginable changes when I did. All of a sudden, the Law of Attraction began working, and I enjoyed prosperity and abundance, health, and a clarity of purpose. Blazing a trail through the dismal forest of low self-esteem, I mapped my process and converted what I had learned into a book called *The Self-Esteem Solution*, which was quickly followed by another book on self-esteem called *R.I.S.E. & Shine,* with daily exercises specific to low self-esteem challenges (such as imposter syndrome, unilateral contracts, Pollyanna thinking, and much more).

And yet . . . I knew I hadn't quite gotten it, that some critical piece of information, some keystone, should be in place that wasn't. Even though, at each juncture, I recognized in myself a greater degree of self-knowledge and self-love, I was compelled to keep searching. I entered and graduated from a seminary with a degree in pre-Christian (Gnostic) theology; I was ordained in Israel as an interfaith minister. I wrote and produced a series of short, direct, practical self-help e-books and self-hypnosis audio files called *Live & Learn Guides,* so that I could break down self-love to a common denominator. So much study, practice, and discipline . . . *what was I missing?*

There's nothing like raw, compassionate self-examination. There's nothing like begging your own mind, the immanent power: *Show me.* The answer came, as many profound answers do, from a totally unexpected source, when I wasn't even looking. An old email resurfaced from a former colleague. At the time he wrote it, my friend Evan was listening to audiobooks from men offering dating advice, and he had forwarded a quote from one of them, "When you die, the Universe dies with you." At the time I thought, "Ridiculous."

Oh, but now I understood!

The only Universe that exists is the one I perceive. When I cease to perceive, it follows that, what I'm perceiving must also cease, because there is nobody there to perceive it.

I formed a new map, through a different, more-mysterious and less-dismal forest. I returned to some early reading with a new intention—to read the word of God as my own word. Here's what I learned, and if asked, the simple ideas I'd want to share with others wherever they are on their journey through life:

- The only authentic tool you have is your perception; understand how to use it and your life is limitless.
- You are the sole agent of change in your life; your universe

exists because of your perception, which you can alter at any time.
- When your ability to perceive the world ceases, your world ceases; imagine the creative position you hold right now!

Looking back, I might have done things differently in the past, but I didn't know what I didn't know. Years ago, my only reference to love was a ten-minute sonogram. Now, because I really consumed, digested, and still grow from a place of conscious perception, I truly get it . . . *we're all one.* Everyone else can only perceive in the same manner that I can: one day at a time, uniquely. We're all composing our own personal songs from the same vast bank of all the musical notes ever written, to which we all have unlimited access.

Life demands I sing my own song, and you yours. It can't be any other way. Now I experience and know subjectively: "I'm awake." And I'm sure I don't know the half of it.

Priscilla Keresey is recognized throughout the country as one of the most accurate, compassionate, and sought-after evidential mediums, connecting the physical and spiritual worlds for individuals and in group demonstrations. She considers herself a practical psychic and enjoys helping her clients achieve their business and personal goals. Priscilla teaches workshops on developing psychic ability and offers training for mediums in her message circles.

Priscilla is certified by the National Guild of Hypnotists as an Advanced Clinical Hypnotist. She created and taught a highly-effective, six-week program on personal empowerment for female inmates in the New York State Correctional System. Priscilla also teaches self-hypnosis to her private clients and in workshops, with a focus on building self-esteem as the first step to all positive change.

Ordained as an interfaith minister in Israel in 2005, Priscilla acts as guest minister at local Spiritualist churches, facilitating services, commitment ceremonies, and funerals. She is a keynote speaker at conferences on the topics of Reclaiming Your Connection to the Divine, Using the Power of Your Inner Mind, and Creating Success & Prosperity.

Priscilla is the author of two books on the Afterlife, *It Will All Make Sense When You're Dead: Messages from Our Loved Ones in the Spirit World* and *Nobody Gets Out of This Alive: More Messages from Our Loved Ones in the Spirit World*.

Her most recent books, *The Self-Esteem Solution: The Breakthrough Plan to Overcome Obstacles, Determine Your Destiny, and Pursue Your Extraordinary Life*, and *R.I.S.E. & Shine: Your Day-by-Day Guidebook to Healthy Self-Esteem*, help readers to recover their inherent self-esteem and start living the life of their dreams. She also wrote the popular *Live & Learn Guides™* series, and is the author and producer of *Live & Learn Guides™* self-hypnosis audio files.

Priscilla lives in New York.

To learn more about Priscilla and her work, visit:

www.apracticalpsychic.com

For inquiries, contact her at: pkeresey@gmail.com

Chapter 15
An Extraordinary Human Life
Heather Hink

Valentine's Day, 2017, is when my life began to fall apart.

Up to that point, my life had been fairly easy. Nothing much to complain about. I had a web design job that I loved, was married with two beautiful kids, and was surrounded by great friends.

Until it all began to slip away.

I was fired from my job on Valentine's Day, which seemed to kick off a major shift in my life. Then, the relationships in my life began to change, to fall apart, and fall away. It felt as if the universe was angry with me. As if I had done something wrong and was being punished for it.

Why was this happening to me? At the time, I didn't understand.

I felt myself being pulled into a state of depression, fearful of what was happening and what was to come. I had discovered the Law of Attraction several years prior to this experience and deeply connected with the concept of using your mind to create the life you desire to experience. I loved to read positive motivational books to help me learn how to live a more happy and fulfilled life experience. Through this avenue of self-help, I discovered Dr. Joe Dispenza, who introduced me to the power of meditation. He teaches people all over the world how to heal themselves and how to gain control of their minds and lives through connecting with the body and going within.

In the meantime, however, I was falling apart. My world was crumbling around me, and I knew that if I didn't get control of my thoughts, feelings, and emotions, I was headed for disaster. So I began to meditate every day. Sometimes twice a day. I found a guided meditation online from Dr. Dispenza, and I listened to it each day, with the intention of clearing my mind and bringing my emotions into balance.

I did this consistently for about a month when one quiet afternoon, I had the most amazing experience. At the time I didn't realize that when you meditate for a period of time and get out of the conscious, thinking mind, you are actively shifting and raising your vibration. You are changing the frequency you hold within your body. This allows you to connect to higher consciousness Beings—your spirit guides and angels.

Now, I didn't know anything about spirit guides and angels during the time I was meditating; I simply wanted to get out of my mind and feel some sort of peace. But the more I meditated, the more I opened the channel for communication with Beings from a higher dimension.

One day as I sat in a semi-darkened room, deep in meditation, I began to see a swirling energy in my mind's eye. I had never seen this energy and wondered what it could be. I watched it swirl and morph into a variety of shapes and patterns. Then, out of nowhere, I had a stream of thoughts that were not my own flow into my mind. I heard, *We are with you, Everything is going to be ok, We love you, We are here for you, We've got you.* On and on, thoughts of love and support streamed through my mind. I wondered for a moment if I was finally losing it and telling myself these things, but I *knew* that these thoughts were not my own.

The knowledge which came through for me that day was that I was connecting with my team of angels who were there to support me through this difficult experience. At that time, I didn't know that angels truly existed. I thought they were only part of biblical times and not here with us now.

This experience began my awakening journey and the discovery that there is so much more to this world and this existence than most of us can even imagine. As everything stable and secure continued to crumble around me, I was guided to learn more about the non-physical world of angels and then, extra-terrestrials.

My guides eased me into the world of Angelics first. They were everywhere! I always seemed to look at the clock at 11:11, 3:33, 5:55 and see angel numbers. Videos of angels would magically appear on YouTube. Recommended angel books would appear under my Audible account without searching for them. Netflix would suggest angel documentaries for me to watch. The angels were trying to get my attention and they did.

As I began to accept that angels exist in our current reality and that I was channeling them during meditation, I was led to the next part of my journey, which was understanding that we are not as alone as we believe ourselves to be on this planet. Not by a long shot. I started to understand that our galaxy is teaming with life of all sorts—a vast array of Beings that live across the universe, some benevolent and some of a darker nature.

Why can't we see these Beings, you might wonder? Why don't more of us know they exist? I think there are many reasons, but one is because they exist in dimensions outside of our own. They are around us but living in a different frequency than we live in. Think of it like a radio station. If you are tuned into one station, you are only able to hear what is being played on that station. Even though you know that other stations exist, you will only hear what is coming through the station you are tuned to.

It is the same for our reality. Earth is tuned to a range of frequencies. We can only physically experience what exists inside that range of frequencies. There is so much more existing around us, but we can't see it or experience it unless we change frequencies or change the station we are tuned into.

This is what is happening now. Many of us are working on raising our frequencies so we can change the station we have been tuned into for so long. Humanity is tired of playing the same games, over and over, that have kept us all trapped in conflict and suffering on this planet, and we are ready to experience life from a higher plane of existence.

This is known as the **Great Awakening**.

My reality began to flood with information, videos, and documentaries, all teaching me about this *awakening* that many of us are moving through at the moment. The deeper I dove into this new knowledge, the more my experience began to make sense. I was waking up and shifting into a new experience, a new reality. I was remembering who and what I truly am.

We have been told for so long that we are simply humans living this one linear human life experience. Many people believe that is all there is—you are born, you live your life, and then you die. Many believe you go to heaven for the rest of eternity; some believe you cease to exist. Then, there is every other belief in between.

But I began to learn that I am a soul, an eternal soul issuing from Source, which you can think of as a vast sea of energy and consciousness that makes up everything in existence. I learned that my soul has lived many physical lifetimes and will continue to live many more after this incarnation is complete.

I also learned that as a soul, I get to choose the experiences I wish to have, including the ability to incarnate as other types of Beings—you know, those Beings that we humans can't see and many have no idea even exist. I have lived as many of those Beings, as have you. Hard to imagine, yet very true.

As my world continued to expand with all of this new and exciting knowledge, I was guided to learn about the Pleiadians, a race of extraterrestrial Beings who originated from the star cluster Pleiades. Just like the angels, information about the Pleiadians began to flood into my reality. I started to feel drawn to work with different energy healers, channelers, and Akashic Records readers, and with each session, I was told over and over that I was Pleiadian.

It can be challenging to accept that you are somehow connected to a race of Beings from another dimension, yet here it was being presented to me with each reading I received. I finally came to accept that I was so much more than this human I believed myself to be, and in that acceptance, I opened up to allow more into my life. So much more.

Along my journey of remembering who I was and why I was here, I found the incredible Dolores Cannon. Dolores seems to pop into your life when you are ready to really begin to understand the true nature of this reality. Her books and videos are incredibly activating and will open your mind in ways you never knew possible.

Dolores was a hypnotherapist who developed her own healing modality known as the Quantum Healing Hypnosis Technique (QHHT®). This modality allows clients to visit past lives and connect to their Higher Selves, or the subconscious mind as Dolores first referred to it, to bring forward knowledge and information to help the client understand what they need to know about their life and how to move forward on their path. This work allowed Dolores to connect with star Beings who channeled higher-dimensional information through her clients. She eventually put that information into many books to share with the world.

I was immediately fascinated with QHHT® sessions and came across several hypnosis practitioners that I felt very drawn to. I spent hours listening to hypnosis sessions shared online, and I was blown away by the information that seemed to effortlessly flow from the mouth of the client under hypnosis. I wanted to know what the magic was behind these sessions and how the practitioner was able to get the client into a state where they could connect with their Higher Selves, their spirit guides, and angels.

That is when I stumbled across Beyond Quantum Healing (BQH) hypnosis and immediately purchased the course. I took the course, learned all the techniques needed to become a hypnosis practitioner, and realized that this was something I wanted to do.

I set up my business and began offering hypnosis sessions to clients all across the world. This work was so exciting, and I enjoyed having the ability to take clients on a journey into what we consider to be past, parallel, and future lives. These sessions also allow the client to voyage into lifetimes as star Beings on other worlds and in other galaxies.

Through my clients, my knowledge and understanding of higher consciousness rapidly expanded and opened me up to so many new experiences. After a year or so as a quantum healing hypnosis practitioner, my work shifted into the realm of spirit and entity release. I began to notice strange things happening with some of my clients that led me to learn about entities and energetic attachments.

As part of this highly energetic world we live in, there are entities and energies that are all around us and at times, can become trapped within our own energy field, creating physical and emotional issues for the person with the attachments. I learned how to clear and release these types of energies from my clients using a method by

Laura Whitworth, founder of Soul Center Healing Hypnosis®. As soon as I began to offer this service, the clients flooded in that needed this type of clearing work.

During my second year as a hypnosis practitioner, I met a client who quickly became a dear friend. Dr. Amelie Biskup is a Natural Functional Medicine Doctor who came in for a session to help her understand some strange things she was seeing with her patients during COVID-19. We began working together and swapping services. She helped me with the physical issues I was experiencing, and I offered her hypnosis sessions in return.

We quickly discovered that she had the gift of channeling and was able to easily connect to a variety of higher-dimensional Beings during her sessions, bringing through incredible information. As her skills became stronger with each session, we realized that we could offer this type of channeling service to clients to help them connect with their galactic guides and angels and receive information from the spirit realm. We created our "Messages from your Guides and Angels" sessions, and Amelie started to channel for clients across the globe. We were blown away by the transformations we were seeing from the clients who received their channeled messages.

Our clients were able to get the information they needed to help them make decisions they had been stuck on for quite some time. Many received the guidance they needed to move forward on their path and their journey through life. They now had the confidence they needed from the information that came through Amelie in these sessions. We could see the expansion in the clients we worked with, and we understood how important these messages truly were.

My own guides began to share with me that part of my role on Earth at this time is to be a bridge between the human realm and the higher dimensions, by offering clients a way to easily connect to their guides and releasing the fear that some have of extra-terrestrial Beings. This work feels so natural to me. I love connecting each week with the star

Beings and the angel teams to bring through powerful messages for our beautiful clients.

One thing about going through an awakening is that you can feel very alone in the process. Many times, your friends, and even family, will fall away because you are no longer in resonance with them. They are unable to understand what you are going through, as they are not on the same path as you.

I recognized this with my clients who felt so alone and at times, a little crazy. I decided to create a platform to host people who needed a space to share the craziest of stories and experiences and feel safe in doing so. I launched the Quantum Soul Portal which is a space where people can feel supported on their awakening journey while receiving ongoing healing through guided quantum meditations, healing, and channeling sessions. The awakening journey is not always a walk in the park, and when you are going through a spiritual awakening, having the support you need is incredibly important.

At this point, my life had become truly exciting! I absolutely loved the work I was doing and the people I was meeting. As I allowed myself to stay open-minded and in the flow of whatever was to come my way, that permitted me to continue to expand the work I was here to do. This is when Starship Healing made its way into my life. My Pleiadian guides began dropping hints to me, during sessions, that I could access a galactic starship and work with the technologies of the starship for healing. When this information first came through I thought, *What on earth are they talking about? This is crazy!* But slowly, they guided me to more information about this concept until eventually, I found a course where this type of connection was being taught. Upon taking the course, I learned the techniques of connecting with a galactic starship for healing and started to consider ways to incorporate this into my work.

Around that time I met my partner, Sarah Huckabee, who came in for a hypnosis session, during which, we discovered that we would be doing this work together. She and I both have an aspect of our soul on a starship, allowing us to easily connect with the healing technologies of the ship and then, provide those frequencies of healing to our clients. We began working with clients, taking them to the starship through quantum healing hypnosis techniques, and were amazed at what we were able to do through this method of healing. My session work began to evolve in the most exciting ways, as more expansive forms of healing took shape.

I have been gifted with two incredible channelers and healers, Sarah and Amelie, and we have combined all of our gifts to create sessions helping our clients experience new ways of energetic healing and connect with their higher guides, angels, and their teams of light. These beautiful ladies bring through powerful messages to remind us all of who we are and why we are here at this time—to help raise the consciousness of this planet so we can all ascend into a higher way of living and being.

Some days I wake up and feel as if I am living in my very own super-hero movie. Once, just an ordinary human girl, who now gets to live an extraordinary life helping people to heal physically and emotion-ally in ways I never imagined possible. I have the honor of speaking with star races from across the Universe and the absolute pleasure of assisting others to connect with their galactic guides and angelic teams.

My awakening journey was not easy. Sometimes I did not think I would make it through. I was one of the ones who chose a "good shak-ing" to wake me up. However, I wouldn't trade that experience for the world, because it moved me out of the ordinary 3-D reality and into a world of pure joy and excitement. I could not be more grateful for this unbelievable experience and I know there is so much more to come!

Heather Hink is a Quantum Healing Hypnosis practitioner who works with clients all around the world to assist them on their journey of healing and their expansion of consciousness.

Heather offers a variety of hypnosis sessions and healing experiences for her clients to choose from including Quantum Healing Hypnosis sessions, Starship Healing Sessions, and guided Quantum Healing Meditations that are channeled through her guides and the Akashic Records.

She works closely with skilled channelers, providing her clients with unique ways of connecting with their galactic guides and angels to receive powerful channeled messages and have access to higher frequencies for healing.

Heather is also the founder of the Quantum Soul Portal, a monthly membership program offering members access to a variety of monthly healing sessions and guided meditations. Members can also attend special channeling sessions to connect with the galactic guides and angels for powerful messages and information. The portal offers a safe space for those on their awakening journey to share their experiences and feel the love and support of a community of loving souls.

You can connect with Heather at www.quantumhealingwithin.com or www.quantumsoulportal.com, where you will find resources to help you on your path of awakening and your journey of healing.

Chapter 16
The Return
Iris Krstanovich

I walk down a grassy path that connects my family's home with a picnic grove belonging to my church. We are custodians of the grove, all forty acres. I know this land and am left alone to wander. It is 1959; I am five years old. On this day, each step on the path reveals what I can now only describe as eternity. To the little girl, it is simply experienced as a rightness of being, a field of joy. I know this because of the zero degrees of separation experienced between nature and my child's body, then known as Stevie. It is as though the sun and trees and grass want me to register the totality of experience which I will spend this lifetime endeavoring to remember and restore. It is my first conscious experience in belonging, so powerful that I am catapulted into a merging with the One.

A few short months later, a series of shattering events occurred, beginning with the destruction of my family house to fire. We moved to inner-city Cleveland. I could not realize that we were all in shock and that parental support systems were unavailable. The shock was compounded one afternoon as I walked my younger brother and myself home from school, one week into this new existence. I could not find our way home. I approached a mailman, and he walked us back to the house. The contrasting worlds of nature and inner city created a rift in my personality. The divine qualities of innocence and purity were submerged, but with nothing to replace them, I no longer had a register for trust. Then began decades of survival in a world that I experienced as bewildering. My foundational memories became deeply embedded in family poverty, maternal and personal depression, paternal, sibling and personal substance abuse, and sibling psychosis. I made choices to survive the overriding of a deep attunement to Source. I withdrew conscious memory of that first, perfect reality revealed to Stevie. Endurance required ways and means more aligned with emotional and physical vigilance. Without a mirror of divine being-ness, ways must be found to exist. Most of these ways are rife with distortion, even as the lost soul parts are contained and preserved until some combination of factors begins their return. This is a story of that return which continues to this day.

My desire is to express this story within the container of alchemical language. Those led to read this contribution may be recovering access to the lost matrices of civilization being restored via collective remembering. I find alchemy to be one such way of recovering access. Our longing is the path to this restoration and return. My heart tells me this is so. Awareness tells me it is possible to remember this access, and words can be alchemical passageways to that end.

What begins is a description of this longing. My personality, now known as Iris, has found its earth experience challenging. I first began looking for comfort by the age of eighteen in metaphysics. Officially a university freshman, yet before the first class commenced, I found myself in a metaphysical bookstore with Stephen Arroyo's, *Astrology, Karma and Transformation,* in hand. I felt strangely secure and trusting in a new path that would give substance to a fearful and ill-equipped personality. There was no recognizable substance to my formative years. Metaphysics offered that substance, an inner-directed way to a truer identity that was not yet being mirrored by people. Then, there was the barest mirror available for those of us who later became the space-holders for the succeeding generations of awakening humans. Nature, to the extent we could access nature, was the space-holder for many of us. This was 1973 after all; we were just beginning to bridge spirit with matter.

This early preparatory period was necessary for the mental, emotional, and physical bodies to gradually awaken over the ensuing decades. The slower nature of time was the container for the way many of us began the return to the soul. Those who moved more quickly experienced more intense spiritual emergencies. Those of us experiencing mental and emotional challenges found that we needed to include the mind in the process. We needed to learn from both the whispers of the soul, and early books and studies, how to see the mental, emotional, and physical bodies as worthy of love. As love began to find its way into the dense layers of human childhood trauma, the intense survival conditioning simultaneously began to release into safety. I now know that trust and safety must be given a place. Trust and safety must matter, especially as the awakening progresses into uncharted areas of this new reality. I see this as a restoration of sacred human architecture. Initially, we assist the individual trauma records, then it is possible to conceive children born into safety. Perhaps, then, future children will not need to remember to awaken! The infant's eyes will gaze into a healing civilization as a mirror of the sacred.

Following the completion of an undergraduate degree, I spent a year in the Northern California wilderness. I learned beginning Acupressure. I immersed in local plant life and wild edibles. I did not know that I was seeking a way into an inner wilderness territory, first revealed to me through the eyes of an inner five-year-old. In my twenties, my understanding of longing was that of belonging to Home. I primarily and intuitively sought the feeling of ecstasy as a pointer, knowing it could be trusted. The early experience of seeking was a difficult contrast to the world upheld by common consensus.

I chose the effort to remember ecstasy over establishing in society. With the exception of a year for additional education, I lived remotely, asking the woods to mirror and teach. During that period, I found a guiding mantra: *I Am divine wilderness.* In holding fast to this mantra, the alchemical power of language began to be revealed. That revelation continues to this day. My ongoing prayer is that the tension of these seeming opposite worlds becomes reconciled. I discover that the mind cannot comprehend the energetic frequency of ecstasy and its ability to shift ages of sorrow, guilt, and fear. I discover that the mind will do anything to retain its mastery over its territory. In this battleground, and I do still consider it a battleground, the witness appears to be ever present. This threshold awareness state, where the reconciliation of opposites is ongoing and exacting in its price, becomes quite an incredible gift to the collective. I tell myself that this gift of reconciliation of opposites is more than enough, for it is born of a new frequency that contains the fire of tension and release.

I have seen the capacity for many of us to shift when language, both alive and sacred, connects with that person for whom the frequency is a match for present time. One of the keys to entering present time where alchemical language is present is to be reverent in our approach to something numinous. We have a register for what that feels like. It will begin to vibrate in response to language that helps us to remember, and return.

My soul is asking me to give voice to the ensuing years of living remotely, primarily in Appalachia. During that time, I met my most precious mentor, a nun living in hermitage in the woods. My personality was then very wild and used to taking defiant oppositional stands. My mentor bi-passed the personality, and we took to meditating in her hermitage instead. She lived non-duality. She introduced me to the mystical Christian classics and then began to hint of her teacher, an Indian master. I was not into masters! That was another of my oppositional stances. On my forty-sixth birthday, he appeared in a lucid dream in my cabin. I am so very grateful for what followed, years of egoic dismantling that culminated in a letting go of decades of multiple substance addictions. The woods became the physical container for a very trying undoing; my mentor's spiritual teacher became the spiritual doula. The trees held space for these massive stages, while all along, transmitting and mirroring their origins as divine Beings, that I might awaken to my original Self.

In that forty-sixth year, my mother died. The woods became everything, even a place to forage for edibles. I surrendered to those woods so that they could accompany the stages of release of distortions that I then assumed were mine. As the distortions began to mentally, emotionally, and physically surface, uninhibited by substances, the body/mind complex knew what to do. I screamed a lot. I walked for miles. I beat rugs on the fence surrounding the cabin. Ancestral work and past and future life clearing converged with the need to sustain integrity as a stellar Being so that greater worlds' missions might be born. Human Iris experienced this time as a series of points of no return, yet was I the one choosing to cross each succeeding threshold? It appears that there are times when we are carried. I was carried, then.

The years in Appalachia transitioned into a calling to world service. I chose to leave the woods and leave behind a constant natural mirror of Source. The need was to turn within, in order to awaken whole brain access. To this day, I believe that the whole brain contains the mirror image of the cosmos. I began to move in this world as if the merging of the two hemispheres was key to accessing life on Earth, life in the stars, and life within. As the commitment to awakening deepened, I also lived the war being waged within me for rational control. As I write this, I remember: When one is born into duality, the brain may both expand in consciousness, in response to the longing to awaken, and continue to participate in the collective consciousness of its time. Is it my compassionate choice on behalf of the collective nesting in a spiritual law? My current offering is that if we stay on Earth as the awakening deepens, we choose to compassionately assist in carrying humanity's burdens. Simultaneously, the love that is released responds in ways beyond comprehension. In the realm of the mystics, life does appear to reveal itself as Mystery. There is an order in this that appears to require awareness of higher law.

The path of spiritual intuition, as service, surfaced when it was time to assist in a more structured manner. Several discarnate teachers presented themselves to offer wisdom and structure in preparations. This assistance was a daily experience for several years. By then, I was older and more discerning of the truth and safety of what was being revealed. Five years later, training ensued in Beyond Quantum Healing (BQH).

As important as that training was, a particular BQH session pointed to an original human memory as it might live within the greater records. The guidance: *to remember and restore the native language of the heart.* It is not a channeled language. It may not be a language at all. It appears to be a perpetual eternal revelatory Source stream, consciously accessible when the heart is present. In this, the language of the heart is unable to be captured or controlled, nor may the mind interpret it. How can the mind capture anything which is perpetually rising from the well of the present? These moments of intersection between the human subject to time and eternity offer maps into the inner realms. New worlds are born in the seething creation flux of these realms, levels of genius we see on this earth that are honored as renaissance eras. Inner knowing states that we are crossing the threshold into such an era. As time itself begins to wobble and warp, conditions are born for freedoms which speak to the lost matrices of paradise. Inner knowing also states that paradise matrices exist—within us, within Gaia, within sentient life.

Nearing the end of this sharing, I wonder: What does the original human hold to be true, and how might that be offered to an anthology on awakening? I believe we were born into an extremely distorted field. To enter incarnation as harmless, thus blameless, is to acknowledge the spiritual incorruptibility of our original humanity. This has been upheld by first nations and those who awakened beyond our conditioned prison. That original human matrix lives in perfect integrity. We remember that the return to this original human matrix is so revolutionary that it might, in and of its own accord, replace the old structures.

I Am present on Earth as one of many, here to remember and return human experience to that of the original human template. I come to recognize the many who are here to remember these paradise states, because we once lived them, and have come again to walk Earth in innocence and safety. The feelings that rise up have been long suppressed, as has been the realm of the sacred feminine. Yet the divine She returns now. We return with Her because the original human lived harmoniously and may be trusted. How do we trust this? We capture a corner of temporal reality in order to make room for the original human to matter, belong, and have a place. When the original human is given a place, the memories are restored. Tantra Maat[1], thank you for your life and awareness on Earth that helps us to remember these and other truths.

I now experience this return through the lens of emergence, that which is revealed after being hidden from view. To that end, the greater realms of which we are a part have been accorded a place here, so that in this incarnation, we might awaken and remember the lost matrices of our ancient civilizations. How have we kept these guideposts of the sacred human available to the journeyer throughout the ages? I believe they are written on our hearts. We can learn to listen with presence to the heart's voice and its myriad ways of communicating truth. This is a sacred calling, spreading as a wildfire

---

1. Tantra Maat is a mystic, seer, prophetess, facilitator of consciousness, and author: https://www.loc-institute.com/

amongst us. As is the way with wildfires, life will renew. I pray that this renewal will reveal the next arm of the sacred spiral of return.

Iris Krstanovich remembers a world once and still here. Knowing tells her that we are simply returning to that world 'still here,' a world that some remember as a paradise. This is her calling, to remember, restore, and return that world via the awakening process. Iris calls this awakening process, emergence. She believes that world is upheld by the ancients, and in present time, by the living records of the first nations on Earth and our own memories recorded in the heart. She personally experiences this return as a disengagement from consensus reality in order to attune to and embody a deeper truth.

To that end, Iris serves as a spiritual intuitive, Beyond Quantum Healing practitioner, group facilitator, and writer. Anchoring all efforts is the knowing that we are held within the soul's alembic as emergent Beings. She has seen that grounding her presence in the heart activates what has always been with us, that world 'still here.' Years living off-grid in the woods gifted her with the silence needed to remember her soul's inner-dimensional gifts: sight, sound, feeling, and knowing.

Iris can be contacted at her website, www.Thelightanddarkofday.com

Her blog musings may be read at www.Emergenceblog.com

Chapter 17
A Ghostly Nightmare
Chrysilla Lewies

Do you believe in the paranormal, Spirits, or life after death?

There is almost always a story to tell when discussing the unknown with others. Statistics now show that fifty percent of people have had some sort of paranormal experience or unexplained event, leaving them perplexed and filled with more questions than answers. These experiences prompt us to question our reality, our life, our purpose, and what happens when we cross over to the Spirit realm.

We are naturally inclined to question and investigate the events in our lives that we don't fully understand. We seek to make sense of them and provide rational, logical explanations. However, when faced with inexplicable and mysterious occurrences, the only logical explanation often points to the presence of something supernatural.

It is believed that children remain connected to the Spirit realm until around the age of seven, as their Spirit has not yet fully integrated into the physical, third-dimensional world. Unlike adults, who often lose this connection through their constant focus on the tangible, children are more attuned to subtle spiritual energy.

Reflecting on my awakening, I trace it back to when I was just seven years old, haunted by a recurring nightmare that never seemed to wane.

We're a small family of four: my parents, my younger sister, and myself. Growing up, we lived in a reasonably large, spacious house. I was blessed with my own bedroom, complete with a small study and an adjoining en-suite bathroom—a setup akin to what South Africans would dub a "granny flat"—I often felt dwarfed by the vastness of my personal space. Perhaps it was merely the innocence of youth that made me uneasy in such a sizable room, or perhaps there lurked something more sinister behind my nocturnal terrors—a truth I would only unearth some thirty years later.

The nightmare began with the image of a young teenage girl, her long brown hair cascading over a rugged dress, standing ominously in the corner of the bathroom. Initially, she appeared benevolent, even friendly, but looming behind her was a sinister black void— an ominous rift that resembled a portal to another realm, ready to swallow anyone who dared to venture inside. The sensation was chilling, as if there was a magnetic force drawing me inevitably towards the darkness. The spectral figure urged me to join her in the ominous portal, and her persistence filled me with an over-whelming dread, leaving a lasting impression of unease and appre-hension.

The nightmare persisted, as I found myself clutching a Bible in one hand, confronting the spectral entity while reciting the Lord's Prayer. With each invocation, she underwent a ghastly transformation. Her innocent expression twisted into a horrifying likeness straight from a horror movie. As the horror intensified, I would inevitably awaken in tears, seeking sanctuary in my parent's bedroom. Their initial annoy-ance at being disturbed from their peaceful slumber only compounded my distress, as they remained skeptical of the vividness and severity of my night terrors.

There were nights when my screams echoed through the house, the terror so intense it felt as though it could rend the very fabric of reality. Yet, my cries fell upon deaf ears, dismissed as mere products of an overactive imagination. I was urged to abandon my fascination for scary movies, but the relentless grip of fear persisted, compelling me to seek solace in the very horrors that haunted my dreams. In an attempt to decipher the inexplicable, I found myself immersed in an endless stream of terrifying films, hoping to glean some understanding from the nightmares that plagued me.

There were nights I would have an open discussion about ghosts and the afterlife with my mother, though I sensed she struggled to grasp the depth of it all. She knew nothing about the supernatural, but one night, while awake, she taught me my first valuable lesson when I asked her about evil Spirits, responding:

> *"Chrysilla, when you allow fear and dread to consume you, you unwittingly invite malevolent forces into your life. Refuse to grant them that power; instead, rely on prayer, for you are always shielded by the hand of God."*

The dreams never really went away, they just opened the door to more questions about death and the afterlife.

Growing up in South Africa, a predominantly Christian country, I found that my curiosity about spiritual matters was often considered taboo. It felt as though my quest to understand it all was placed on hold, particularly until I completed my degree in wholesale and retail travel in 2006. At the age of nineteen, I took matters into my own hands by applying for a working-holiday visa and purchasing a ticket to embark on a journey to live in the United Kingdom.

It took a few years to settle and find my feet, while growing up really quickly. I had to navigate the complexities of opening a bank account, paying taxes and rent, and finding a job in a country where I was deciphering accents—English, Irish, Scottish. And if you think the English speak "proper" English, think again. I quickly learned about Cockney Rhyming Slang, which sounded something like this: *"She is on that dog and bone again."* Confused and feeling more lost than ever, I soon discovered that it simply meant 'phone'—yes, a telephone or mobile phone. Understanding the locals proved to be a challenge in itself, especially since Afrikaans is my first language, not English, let alone Cockney Rhyming Slang.

In 2012, during what some refer to as the *great awakening*, I found myself being pulled back into the unresolved questions stemming from my childhood nightmares. Driven by intuition, I sought answers and embarked on a journey of exploration. This quest led me to Haunted Happenings (a group that organizes overnight ghost hunts and ghost tours), where I made the bold decision to attend my first ghostly event—a visit to Kelvedon Hatch, nestled in the heart of Brentwood, Essex. This site, once a Cold War-era Nuclear Bunker, lay buried 125 feet (38 meters) beneath the Earth's surface.

As I stepped into the bunker, I felt a surge of excitement, knowing I was about to embark on an extraordinary journey. It was there that I encountered my very first psychic medium. I couldn't help but blush with embarrassment as I asked her, "Are you a medium?" With a warm smile, she replied, "No, I'm a small," and we shared a light-hearted chuckle, a question that I'm sure she's been asked many times before. Little did I know, this encounter was about to open not just a door but an entire Pandora's box of revelations.

I never really saw myself as a tech geek, but I've always had a soft spot for quirky gadgets, especially ones with a supernatural twist. That's how I stumbled upon the Spirit Box—a device that intrigued me from the get-go. Essentially, it's like a radio scanner that cycles through frequencies, generating white noise.

The fascinating part?

Many believe Spirit can manipulate this noise to communicate and answer questions. Alongside the Spirit Box, I delved into the world of digital recorders, which capture Electronic Voice Phenomena (EVP) —a phenomenon where ghosts or spirits leave behind auditory imprints of their presence.

While experimenting with gadgets, I also delved into more traditional tools, such as the Ouija board and table tipping. However, it wasn't just about playing around with these devices; I was taught to approach them with respect, opening and closing sessions with prayer. As you might expect, these practices are often considered a no-go in Christian circles, and they're certainly not for the faint of heart.

One of my most memorable Spirit Box sessions occurred during a lunch break in an empty meeting room at work. I was alone, and to my surprise, a clear and distinct voice came through the Spirit Box, saying, "I love you." It was unlike anything I had experienced before; the voice was unmistakable. Intrigued, I engaged in conversation with the entity, asking for its name. It responded, "Reece." When I inquired about how he passed, the response was chillingly brief: "scaffolding." The energy in the room was palpable, enough to send shivers down anyone's spine.

Despite my efforts, I couldn't uncover any records of scaffolding accidents or a person named Reece meeting their end at this location. Nevertheless, I always make a point to investigate thoroughly.

My Spirit Box became my travel companion, accompanying me on various adventures—from eerie visits to cemeteries to cruising the Mediterranean. I remember thinking, *there'll be no shortage of ghosts on that cruise ship.* Fortunately, I had a partner who shared my open-mindedness and was willing to explore the unknown alongside me. Sometimes, his curiosity led him to join me on my ventures, as we searched for answers to the mysteries of the afterlife. Besides, he wasn't about to let me wander into creepy cemeteries all by myself—he was simply being a gentleman by accompanying me.

One late night in the cemetery, my partner and I found ourselves standing amidst the gravestones, seemingly talking to thin air like a couple of "crazies," all in hopes of capturing EVPs on our digital recorder. Suddenly, out of nowhere, there was a loud thud. We were petrified, and we took off running, feeling like mischievous children caught in the act. I can laugh about it now, but I will caution everyone dabbling with gadgets in such environments.

I was always told to be afraid and was cautioned about all the evil that's out there in the world of Spirit, but honestly, I feel we have more to be afraid of in the world of the living than the dead. While I have encountered some negative energy, I believe it's crucial to approach it with caution. If I sense an energy that feels "not so good," I promptly cease communication and offer prayers for them to find peace and light.

I believe that we often scare ourselves more than the latter—Spirits scaring us. Take, for instance, our venture into the cemetery. We found ourselves in a place where we weren't supposed to be, experimenting with things we didn't fully comprehend. That alone is enough to instill fear in anyone.

It all builds character, though, and everything is a learning curve. Slowly but surely, these experiences transformed my life, becoming an integral part of who I am. Despite my love for visiting haunted places, I couldn't shake the feeling that there was something more I was meant to do. Undeterred, I pressed on with my quest to unravel the mysteries of energy, consciousness, and the afterlife. This journey eventually led me to join a development circle with four others; we met weekly for two years.

It's common knowledge that humans have five senses, in addition to a "sixth sense" that is sometimes referred to when dealing with *the unseen.* When connecting with Spirit, the members of our circle also tapped into these senses:

- Clairvoyance (clear seeing)
- Clairaudience (clear hearing)
- Clairsentience (clear feeling)
- Claircognizance (clear knowing)
- Clairalience (clear smelling)
- Clairgustance (clear tasting)

We're all unique individuals, which means we each perceive the world through our senses differently. In our development circle, we learned how to attune to those senses and understand how they present within us. We were taught to connect with Spirit and discern between our own sensations and the messages received from the Spirit world. Sometimes, we utilized various tools such as meditation, colored ribbons, automatic writing, or psychometry to enhance our connection with Spirit. It's fascinating how methods like these have been used throughout history, reminiscent of Nostradamus gazing into a bowl of water infused with herbs to make his predictions.

We shift our focus from our analytical left hemisphere to the intuitive right hemisphere. In this space, we're able to perceive patterns, make connections, and even read people like an open book.

We all possess this divine gift—a journey of internal reflection intertwined with the cultivation of empathy and understanding of the Spirit realm when conveying messages to loved ones or clients. Additionally, under UK law, there are numerous rules to adhere to, legally speaking; we are accountable for the messages we deliver.

We're cautious not to overstep boundaries in our practice. We refrain from diagnosing medical conditions, prescribing medications or diets, and predicting pregnancies. Imagine the disappointment of spending thousands of pounds on clothing and accessories, expecting a baby boy, only to be met with a surprise of the opposite. There's no *oops* that can fix that.

In 2014, I stumbled upon Dolores Cannon quite unexpectedly. It was one of her *inner Earth* videos that initially caught my attention, where she discussed the fascinating realm of *Elementals*[1]. Intrigued, I found myself captivated by her insights and wisdom as I delved deeper into her work. Later that day, I decided to learn more about this remarkable woman. To my delight, I discovered that she would be visiting London in just a few weeks' time. It felt like serendipity, and without hesitation, I booked a ticket to attend her event.

Upon meeting her, she advised that I needed no professional college or university degrees to become a Quantum Healing Hypnosis Technique (QHHT®) practitioner. It felt like the day was just getting better and better.

I gathered the funds and eagerly signed up to become a Level 1 QHHT® practitioner. It was a pivotal moment; I felt like I was finally discovering my purpose in life, all at the age of twenty-seven. Building on that foundation, I progressed to become a Level 2 practitioner just a year later, and from that point on, I never looked back

I'm also trained in Beyond Quantum Healing (BQH). With BQH, we focus on the concept of the Higher Self—an aspect of ourselves that possesses profound wisdom and insight. It's like being at the base of a mountain while our Higher Self stands atop, offering a panoramic view of our lives. Through BQH, we can access answers to questions about our life's purpose, the significance of certain relationships, or the reasons behind their breakdown. It's through this practice that I learned the profound truth of our interconnectedness.

I cannot hurt you without hurting myself. And through helping you, I

---

1. Elementals are thought to be spirit Beings, such as elves, gnomes, water sprites, mermaids, and fae, that exist in a dimension other than our third dimension.

am also learning and developing my own soul's growth, under-standing the web of consciousness we are all part of.

My spiritual journey didn't end with Quantum Healing. Did you know that the United Kingdom has its own modern-day Hogwarts? I've had the privilege of studying mental mediumship and trans-mediumship at the Arthur Findlay College—a renowned institution dedicated to Spiritualism and psychic science. It's a melting pot of knowledge, drawing people from all corners of the globe.

There's a profound depth to Spiritualism that reveals itself when you fully dedicate your life to working with Spirit.

Bringing This Full Circle

During a return trip to South Africa in 2023, while discussing my night terrors with my parents, they casually mentioned that the house had been used for church gatherings, as it was owned by a priest. This revelation left me wondering: What were these gatherings about? What truly transpired in my room, dubbed the "granny flat?" Unfortunately, we may never uncover the answers to these lingering questions.

It's been an exhilarating journey, although at times, quite solitary. While we can seek support from others, ultimately, we must walk this path alone. Therefore, it became paramount for me to surround myself with like-minded individuals wherever possible.

I'm now thirty-seven, and as you can see, I've truly worked my way up from the bottom. This journey is just a glimpse into my awakening story, but I hope it serves as a reminder that with dedication, anything is possible. May it offer some inspiration along your own path.

When asked who has influenced me and my work, I find it difficult to name just one individual. Throughout my life, I've been fortunate to have many mentors who have left a lasting impact on me. As Lao Tzu beautifully said, "When the student is ready, the teacher will appear.

When the student is *truly* ready, the teacher will disappear." Each mentor has played a crucial role in guiding me along my journey of growth and development.

Transitioning from being scared of the dark and plagued by nightmares to confidently connecting with Spirit has been a transformative journey for me, one that now involves helping others find their purpose, as well.

I've learned that whether we use Tarot cards or psychometry, they are simply tools, and it's the intention behind their use that matters most —to serve the highest good for all. With daily prayer and the unwavering belief in divine protection, I've been guided throughout my life's path. Now, I am honored to share my experiences and teachings with others.

Spirit isn't seeking your ability, but your availability. If you make the effort to work with them, they will undoubtedly show up.

Chrysilla Lewies was born in South Africa and raised in Florida, Roodepoort, a quaint town nestled in the suburbs of Johannesburg. Her spiritual journey began with dreams in her childhood, sparking a curiosity that stayed with her until the time was right to delve deeper.

At nineteen, she embarked on a transformative journey to the United Kingdom, where she devoted herself to the exploration of Spirit and the principles of Spiritualism. Under the expert guidance of renowned mentors at the prestigious Arthur Findlay College in Stansted, London, Chrysilla honed her skills as a mental and trans-medium.

In 2012, her interest in the afterlife and communication with Spirit led her to Dolores Cannon, where she qualified as a QHHT® practitioner. She also trained in Beyond Quantum Healing BQH and Quantum Connect. These skills have allowed her to explore her clients' life patterns, blocks, and their connections to past lives within the intricate web of consciousness.

Early in her spiritual development, Chrysilla discovered the Spiritualist National Union, where she remains an active member. Her dedication and hard work have earned her the title of international medium, giving her the privilege to travel to Montreal, Canada and the United States to demonstrate her gift of mediumship and communicate with Spirit.

In addition, Chrysilla enjoys writing and publishing her own articles, often contributing to Elephant Journal and participating in the Elephant Journal Academy.

Connect with Chrysilla directly at www.chrysillalewies.com

Chapter 18
A Second Wave Soul
Kathleen Isenhart, RN

"We will come back for you," the tall, thin, gray male Being said. "You are on a mission here."

"But," I exclaimed, "I don't want to stay here! I want to go back there. These humans aren't mine; I am tall, thin, and gray, too!"

He firmly replied, "No, not yet. You can do it; you can stay here! You will be fine, and the Crystal Flame Being [my guide] will stay here with you. You are strong . . . you can do this! I will always be with you."

I cried, though I knew he was right . . . I *had* agreed to this mission. He smiled, hugging me. I felt so safe in his presence. Then, he retreated to the ship, while the Crystal Flame Being tucked me into bed.

I was seven years old.

I emerged from this Beyond Quantum Healing (BQH) hypnosis session still crying. "How do you feel?" the hypnotist asked. "Relieved. Relieved and very sad," I responded. In the weeks that followed, as I processed this and the prior hypnosis sessions, there was a theme in the regressions—the story of my life was finally making sense.

I do not feel like I fit in this world but rather, watch as an outsider. I enjoy being alone. I am uncomfortable around larger groups of people, preferring to be with one to a few at a given time. I love to read. I did not believe in a god, as described by human religions, believing, instead, that we are purely the product of "evolution." I had no real passion, no vision or plan for my own future. Life appeared to be a series of unplanned, unrelated events, to which I would respond . . . *Ok, I will try that.* I became angry at how humanity, which included myself, could be violent and untruthful, blatantly disregarding nature and Mother Earth. As one person, I wondered how could I make a difference when I, too, was a part of the problem. I became frustrated by social injustice. Because I love *Star Trek*, the original series, I would often find myself thinking: *Beam me up Scotty, there is no intelligent life here.* Life appeared a series of tasks. This world did not make sense. Why was I here? Clearly, I did not enjoy being here.

After the death of a dear family member due to cancer, in 2003, I discovered Louise Hay's book, *You Can Heal Your Life*, the Hay House "I Can Do It" conferences, Abraham Hicks and the Law of Attraction material, as well as many other alternative health and metaphysical authors and practitioners. My family member's death rattled me—she was only in her early thirties. She had undergone surgery, chemotherapy, radiation, and a bone marrow transplant to arrest the cancer, which had not brought success, only suffering. As I delved into the metaphysical material, I just could not believe—was not ready to believe—that we, or she, or anyone would create their own illness or that we, conversely, could *reverse* said illness. You see, I was, and still am, a registered nurse, thoroughly trained in the traditional western medicine perspective. Having dropped out of college years before, due to a fear of writing, I entered nursing school at the suggestion of my insightful mother.

I loved my years as a bedside nurse, practicing alongside so many compassionate, caring individuals and working as a team to help those entrusted to our care. I have a healer's heart, I realized. Unfortunately, while we seemed able to assist in the recovery of various traumatic injuries, to a degree, we were not really *healing* anyone suffering from chronic conditions—cancer, diabetes, thyroid disease, obesity, anxiety, depression, osteoporosis, heart failure, and many other conditions that seemed ubiquitous in our patient population. Instead, we treated symptoms and delayed death. In fact, it felt like, in some cases, we were actually causing harm. Our interventions to "save" and "treat" were painful, as many patients will tell you. Simply placing an intravenous line is a painful procedure. Moreover, what was considered usual or best practice in my early nursing years was eventually reconsidered, labeled harmful, and replaced by new, "evidence-based" practices.

Even my *own* chronic, bodily symptoms continued to worsen despite prescribed care. Still not convinced that my energetic thoughts and feelings could be the source of my symptoms, I sought care from western-medicine providers and alternative medicine practitioners, ingested hundreds of supplements, and followed a variety of recommended diets. I spent thousands of dollars—nothing worked. I became disillusioned with the benefits of *any* medical advice and left bedside nursing. I did not leave the practice of nursing; I merely changed venues.

By 2013, higher guidance was leaking through, nudging me to reinvent myself as a legal nurse consultant (LNC), defending fellow nurses against claims of medical and nursing negligence. I didn't view this as a conflict (separating myself from traditional medicine while continuing to work in that arena), because those practitioners' hearts and intentions are good.

They are caring and compassionate, with the desire to heal and cure, just like me. Perhaps their tools are archaic, but that is their current level of healing knowledge. Our world is not yet ready to completely eliminate this branch of healing medicine. And practically speaking, I still needed a career and an income. At this point I was not yet fully "awakened." As we know, every experience is valuable—through the opportunities presented as an LNC, under the tutelage of my brilliant defense attorney (who is, himself, a gifted writer) and our defense team, I am learning to write, to articulate my thoughts, to grow. In fact, this experience has given me the confidence to write this chapter for you, dear readers.

In 2015, I discovered Dr. Steven Greer and his Disclosure Project, learning that governments have not only been aware of but have been covering up contact with extraterrestrials since the 1940's. I traveled on a CE5 expedition[1] with his group, where we contacted two extraterrestrial vehicles hovering above the east coast of Florida. Talk about stretching the belief boxes I existed in!

All of this metaphysical and extraterrestrial information was inconsistent with what I had learned through years of schooling, not to mention with mainstream beliefs. History, science, the "laws" of the universe, and evolution were not the entire truth or even close to the truth? Higher Beings have been lovingly guiding and teaching humanity all along? There is a higher power, a Source of all? And it is pure love? We are not a physical body, but rather, we are a soul having a physical experience? Our consciousness, our soul, never dies? Thoughts are *things, energy*? Love is the most powerful guiding emotion of intent when manifesting? This reality is actually the dream?

---

1. Close Encounters of the 5th Kind Expedition: Participants utilize CE-5 protocols to actively engage in mutual bilateral contact with extraterrestrial intelligence while in a state of cosmic consciousness, vectoring them to the group's location on Earth for a peaceful encounter and cooperative communication (drstevengreer.com).

What information could I trust as "true?" What is the truth? *Is there* a truth?

In early 2023, I reached a crisis point. I had received a diagnosis of thyroid cancer in 2020 and was being told by western medicine practitioners that it was incurable. We were now three years into the pandemic, with fear running rampant, and I had just suffered through the loss of two of my dogs. I was beyond stressed—I was in a state of fear and anger. I was not enjoying life. The *whys* had not been answered. Truth seemed ever more elusive. I told my husband something had to change. I don't know what it was to be, but something had to shift.

And it was *something*, all right.

Something lifesaving *and* life altering. In May of 2023, while online, researching extraterrestrials and Earth, I came across an article that discussed Dolores Cannon and her extensive work. Intrigued, I immediately went to her website. I immersed myself in her books and extensive YouTube videos—interviews, talks, and her *Metaphysical Hour* episodes. The information she presented—obtained through thousands of individual hypnosis sessions, during which, she spoke to her clients' "subconscious" (the SC, as she called it)—reiterated and coalesced so much of the information I had been reading about for decades from so many diverse authors and disciplines.

Through her work, I learned about the real cause of illness, God, extraterrestrials, humanity's hybrid history, consciousness, energy, and vibration, as well as the concept that we are all *one collective*, each presenting as an aspect of Source, having individual physical experiences. I felt such relief yet found myself with even more questions. Importantly, Dolores developed a reproducible process, called Quantum Healing Hypnosis Technique (QHHT®), to connect her clients to their Higher Selves (the SC), and/or Source, for an explanation of their current issues, for guidance, or (most critically) for self-healing. For me, her work affirmed that all of our answers, including how to heal, are within us, because we are beautifully connected to a loving Source, the creator of all there is. I was, at that time, an unsuccessful meditator . . . I wanted to, *had to*, experience that connectedness.

I scheduled my first QHHT® session for July of 2023. I was very emotional during the interview portion—that, alone, was cathartic, because it felt like "coming home," communicating with someone I felt safe to share my most private thoughts and fears with. The hypnosis portion was a bust, however. My conscious mind would not relent. I was the dreaded "left brained" client. But as we know, everything always works out as it should. As it turns out, the hypnotist was a channeler; she channeled her guides so I could obtain the answers to my questions.

What did they tell me? They told me, "No, they would not answer any of my questions." They lovingly explained that I needed to deal with my anger and fear first. I must learn to meditate, visualize, and engage in self-reflection. And I needed to speak my truth. I had no idea what that meant! Subsequently, I learned that, energetically, the general cause of cancer is related to anger . . . extreme anger at Self. And throat related cancers, i.e., thyroid cancers? Not speaking up for yourself, not speaking your truth, and stifled creativity. The hypnosis practitioner offered to have me return for another session, since technically, this one was not completed. She was fantastic, patient, compassionate, gifted, and professional.

I met with her again in October of 2023. My consciousness continued to create blocks during the session, but the practitioner navigated those blocks expertly, assuring me I was doing fine . . . that we were getting answers and to trust the first thought I had. I did not go to a past life. Rather, I was a tall, grey, humanoid Being, standing alone on some type of material made of iridescent stone, raising my arms, and sending waves of loving, joyous energy upwards and outwards. Oh, it was a glorious feeling! For over a year prior to this session, I had been having nighttime and daytime dreams . . . dreams that I was a huge Being, standing on the Earth, raising my arms skywards and sending flames of loving, joyous, yellow, light energy around the Earth. Coincidence? Unlikely.

The practitioner then explored, via the subconscious (SC), my concerns related to my cancer diagnosis. Below, is an excerpt from the session.

Hypnotist: What is happening in Kathleen's neck?

SC: Lots of pressure in my neck.

Hypnotist: What has made Kathleen emotional?

SC: Fear that there is something wrong.

Hypnotist: Why is there such fear?

SC: Because initially, she was told there was. Then, they removed something that supposedly was bad. Then, they said it was still there. So she still believes it is still there.

Hypnotist: What is below that fear?

SC: That maybe she really does not want to be in this life.

Hypnotist: Why is that a fear?

SC: Aren't we supposed to want to be here? Maybe it is her time to go. She doesn't know which it is, to stay or go.

Hypnotist: So how does the thought of going feel like?

SC: Escaping and relieving at the same time.

Hypnotist: Why doesn't Kathleen want to be here?

SC: Seems like it is a lot of work. It has good things, but humanity is not a good thing. We can't move forward. Feels like work. It is not fun.

Hypnotist: What are you doing on the throat? Is there anything there you need to look at?

SC: I think so.

Hypnotist: What is the cause of the pressure in the throat area?

SC: Pressure on either side. Under the jawline.

Hypnotist: Are you doing any work on the throat area?

SC: Yes.

Hypnotist: How are you healing it?

SC: There is nothing there, I got rid of it. The pressure will be gone.

The SC explained that I was shown the gray Being in order to experience *joy*. The gray Being was happy doing what it was doing. I could follow that example and just *enjoy being . . . enjoy being and sharing the energy . . . joy is enough.* Why? Because I was always trying to *do* something. It was suggested that I *just be . . . let go . . . and trust*—trust in Source, listen to and trust the guidance of my Higher Self, trying to break into my awareness. The SC said, of the cancer, *we got rid of it,* while releasing the fear from my heart.

This was a momentous experience for me! I felt a wave of relief with the release of the fear of "cancer." My dreams were validated. I realized, in that moment, that all my answers are within me, and I am able to *access* those answers. Some aspect of me is a non-human Being—this human form is not all that I am. And my Higher Self was confirming that my thoughts and beliefs were powerful energies that could manifest illness or help me to heal. And there was even more enlightenment to come.

The next week I signed up for QHHT® training—this was my healing calling. I wanted to be a hypnotist. To facilitate sessions in which others could access their Higher Selves, their inner knowing, and their self-healing . . . to offer others the experience and gift I was

given. I could not learn fast enough! I connected with others, swapping practice sessions. One practitioner suggested I try a Beyond
Quantum Healing (BQH) hypnosis session. *What was this BQH?* I
thought to myself. Again, I immediately investigated. The first thing I
saw on the BQH website was the logo, a cardinal. Unreal! I had been
decorating my home with cardinals for the previous two years. What
a sign! I signed up for BQH training that very day. Surprisingly, it
dawned upon me, that same day, that the first line of the QHHT®
induction is, "See a red bird."

Two amazing BQH sessions brought further insight. During the first
session, my guide, a gorgeous, pure black stallion, galloped with me,
bareback, at lightning speed, through the nothingness, with no destination. The ride was thrilling, exciting, and fun! Mind you, I do not
like riding horses; I've ridden three times and was very unsettled each
time. But this ride was freeing! The lesson and purpose? To "enjoy
the ride" of this life. Which brings us to the second session and the
beginning of this chapter. When I was seven years old, I was
reminded that I had agreed to this mission in human form. I had a
mission, and I had to complete it. I *volunteered* to be here. Enlightenment dawned! The cancer was anger at my physical body, because I
did not want to *be in* this body. To speak my truth, as I was
instructed, means to speak *love* to my body, thanking and appreciating it for allowing me to fulfill my mission. And to share my truth
with others.

What is my mission? I believe I am a second wave volunteer, as
described in Dolores Cannon's book, *The Three Waves of Volun-
teers and the New Earth*—here to change the energy of the Earth
and help raise humanity's vibration, so we may ascend with Earth
to the fifth dimension. These "second wavers" are *antennas*,
beacons, generators, channels of energy. We don't have to *do*
anything, we just have to *be*. Dolores explains that the "second
wavers" don't really feel comfortable around people, even though
our job is to affect people, via our energy. This creates a paradox.

We prefer to be observers rather than participants—to do our job and *get out.*

As a Second Wave Soul, I volunteered to be here in this physical body on Earth at this time. This body is not all that I am. In this body, my mission, as I now know it consciously, is to *be* and *enjoy being and sharing the energy* with humanity and planet Earth, wherever I am, for as long as I am to be here. The possibilities and opportunities to help others is endless. As both a both a QHHT® and BQH practitioner, I thrive on sharing the love and joy with each individual I come in contact with, facilitating their journey of enlightenment and healing through connection to the all loving Source. My journey continues, and I am, finally, learning to "enjoy the ride."

Kathleen Isenhart's own hypnosis sessions provided insights and healing that were life altering and lifesaving; for this reason, she is thrilled to have become both a QHHT® and BQH hypnosis trained practitioner. In retrospect, Kathleen understands that Source guided, and she manifested, the experiences that encouraged her own spiritual awakening.

Kathleen grew up in beautiful Rochester, New York. She loved playing soccer, becoming captain of her high school and college soccer teams. She has been a practicing registered nurse for over thirty-four years, in various venues, currently working as a legal nurse consultant.

In the early 2000's Kathleen relocated to sunny Tampa, Florida. There, Source connected her with her love and best friend, whom she married in 2012. Between them, they have seven children, six grandchildren (and counting), and one great-grandchild. Her family and amazingly loving husband are her foundation . . . the backbone, the scaffolding upon which her journey of life is possible. They love, support, guide, and forgive without judgement. Absent any one of them, Kathleen would not be Kathleen.

Connect with Kathleen directly at YEShypnoses@outlook.com or visit www.YEShypnoses.com

Chapter 19
The Day I Saw Red
Kristina Skirving, RMT

In summer 2011, I accidentally saw an intimate text message from a woman to my husband. I read through the entire thread. Rage swelled inside me. My eyes saw red . . . literally. I walked, body shaking, to the back corner of our property and screamed like a banshee. Then, a calmness washed over me, and my mind was clear.

The red, the rage, and the scream was a rebirth. It was this Scorpio's rising of the Phoenix. In the few minutes standing in the backyard, the years of his narcissistic abuse and manipulation became crystal clear. A veil had been lifted. I felt an inner strength I had never known. The healing had begun. I went back in the house and acted as if nothing had happened. The next weekday, I called an attorney and subsequently, filed for divorce. I, then, repaired my relationship with my son, family, and friends.

I told myself I would never succumb to another narcissistic relationship, but how wrong I was. Back then, I didn't have the language or tools to recognize "love bombing" or other narcissistic traits, and so, I married again, exactly two years after my first divorce was finalized. A negative shift in the relationship occurred the day after we wed.

Within a year, I recognized the familiar red flags and caught his infidelity in 2015. This time, however, I had the strength to stand up for myself. He had no power over me. I moved into a spare bedroom, creating and executing an exit plan. It would take time—years in fact—but I knew from the experience of my first marriage that I could do it.

In addition to the exit plan, I began to work on my own healing. I asked myself how I could have fallen for this type of relationship *again*. Reflecting on my life, I realized that most of my romantic relationships had been abusive. I had to figure out why I was drawn to that type of man—I needed to do the *shadow work*. I determined that the only way to break this cycle was to go within and heal myself spiritually. But I was unsure how to do it.

I discovered that a former co-worker and his wife, already on their ascension path, were Reiki practitioners. I had never heard of Reiki, but I was desperate to heal, so I signed up for a session with them in the fall of 2018. I felt completely different afterwards. It changed my life! As Reiki Master teachers, they offered Reiki classes, as well, so I signed up for the Level 1 course in May, 2019.

Prior to the *attunement* (a sacred ritual in which the Reiki Master connects the student to the source of Reiki), I was led through a guided meditation where we were to meet a spirit guide. The meditation took us to a mountain top clearing, where there was a fire surrounded by large sitting stones. During the meditation, I saw a big burly man, with a long red beard and patch over his right eye, approach from another path. He was wearing a long, belted shirt and leggings made of animal skin, fur boots on his feet, and his shoulders were wrapped in a gray wolf fur. This man entered the clearing and sat near me. His name was Odin. We sat for a moment, and then, he handed me a brightly glowing, white crystal cluster. I brought the crystal cluster to my chest, where it infused with my heart chakra. Odin, then, stood up and walked back to his path, into the darkness.

After the meditation was the attunement, which literally opened the entire universe to me! I felt Odin's presence, once again, when I called him in to be near me during my first (practice) Reiki session that day. I was not surprised that Odin was my guide; rather, I was quite pleased, as my ancestral heritage is Celtic Scottish.

Reiki was the first step of my ascension, and I know that I was divinely guided to it. I continued taking classes, eventually achieving Reiki Master teacher two years later. Feeling the love of Source, through Reiki, set me on my path of healing, discovery, and evolution.

Quantum Timeline Healing (QTH) was another modality that was recommended to me. My first session in December, 2021 was extremely beneficial and enlightening. Through a past-life clearing, I learned that my lesson in *this* lifetime is fear of abandonment, the discovery of which enabled me to address and heal this subconscious fear. As I reflected on the major traumas of my life, particularly during childhood, it became evident how they affected my intimate relationship choices. That underlying fear made me easy prey for narcissists. The QTH practitioner also cleared other lifetimes that presented themselves, cut a negative energetic cord, removed two energetic parasites, repaired and energized the crystalline pathways in my brain, and informed me that I had been a healer in most of my past lives. Through these processes, I gained a deeper understanding of myself.

Of particular interest, regarding the cord that was cut . . . it was from my first husband. We had existed in several lifetimes together—not solely as man and wife—most of which ended badly. In our first life together, he blamed me for his death and cursed me, which created the energetic cord. In each lifetime together after that, his curse brought me pain and suffering. No more! I actually felt the snap in my energetic body when she cut the cord. In fact, I could physically feel all the energy work she performed. I felt so much lighter, happier, and free! My mind was clearer and energy flowed much easier.

A journey with plant medicine in February, 2022 allowed me to float in the heavenly love of Source and see my true identity as a *divine Being,* having a human experience. The journey was surreal. I was floating in space with twinkling stars and colors swirling around, like the aurora borealis, primarily in fuchsia pink and green. A bright, white light appeared with five shadowed Beings beckoning me. As I drew closer, I recognized one as Odin; these were my guides. One was an owl. I asked his name, and he politely said it was not something I could pronounce as a human. He told me to call him Grandpa. A third was a very handsome man with black hair, graying at the temples, steel blue eyes lined with thick, black lashes, and a chiseled jaw. I felt a very strong connection with him. His name was John.

I asked my guides to show me what I needed to know, because I was not sure how to navigate this space. A small bolt of lightning, compliments of Odin, appeared off to the left, so I floated towards it. Another bright light appeared, and I traversed into a lifetime scene. I continued to follow the lightning bolts to other lifetimes, all of which were abandonment themed. These scenes showed me specific events to focus on in order to continue healing. This experience also taught me how to *purposely* journey via lucid dreaming—interestingly, I have always done this without understanding what it was, but now I could do it at will. I will never forget waking up from a lucid dream once, just as my light body was entering back into my physical body. It was a beautiful, glowing gold color. Once it had fully reintegrated, my aura glowed gold briefly, after which, I returned to my physical body awareness.

A surrogate Beyond Quantum Healing (BQH) session in May, 2022, again on recommendation, was another incredible experience. It was conducted by two practitioners who are also sisters: one served as my surrogate, while the other facilitated the session. Prior to the session, I submitted questions for them to investigate. First, the surrogate practitioner was taken to a city named Helios, which exists on a sun in our universe—we see it as a star from Earth—where there was an ornate, gold pyramid that was larger, even, than Cheops, the Great Pyramid of Giza. Helios is populated primarily by Lyran white lion Beings and very tall, slender, humanoid shaped, ancient, translucent white light Beings. My Helios support team included three Lyrans, all soul friends of mine, and a sun archangel connected directly to me, named Honipshet.

After learning, in my QTH session, that I carried ancient healing knowledge, one of my questions for this session had been to ask for more information and guidance on this topic. I learned that I am an energy fractal of one of the ancient, white light Beings on Helios, who is a healer to its kind. As I continue to incarnate into lifetimes as a healer, my knowledge and experiences are conveyed to the ancient white light Being.

During my BQH session, I acquired detailed information about my lives as a female healer in Lemuria and Egypt. I was told which ancient gifts are accessible to me now, given tools to develop and access them, and provided with locations on Earth where I could travel to further my healing and spiritual awakening. The most helpful gift I carry now is the gift of divine femininity—this gift is paramount in the great awakening and transition to the New Earth. I learned that assisting others with this transition is also in my contract. As a bonus, I found that the cause of my chronic back pain was confirmed to be from a past life trauma.

In September, 2022, I participated in a group regression / stream of consciousness session with my BQH practitioners. Participants asked questions of our guides, and we wrote their answers as they came, similar to a channeled writing process. Curious of the connection between Source, the galactics, and myself, I asked for clarification.

The response was that I had been a Lyran in a previous galactic life. Two of the Lyran soul friends from Helios and I had traveled space together. That explained why I have always been drawn to and felt a deep connection with the cosmos. I am, in fact, a Lyran starseed. I came to understand that Source created *all* universal Beings; therefore, we are all connected.

Lastly, I asked if there was anything else my guides wanted to communicate to me during this session. They responded:

> *"Be strong, happy, love again; John is coming, allow his light into your life; Scotland, two years."*

Bam! Now I understood the strong connection to John during the plant medicine journey. He is not a guide. Rather, my guides were bringing him into my awareness. After a lifetime of failed intimate relationships, I had given up. I felt unworthy of a truly loving relationship. I was wrong! I do not believe John would have been brought into my awareness otherwise. This brought a great deal of hope and peace to my heart, as well motivation to heal more.

My second QTH session in October, 2023 cleared even more lifetimes and brought forth more incredible information. One of my questions concerned my forever partner. Without any prompting from me, the practitioner described him to me and then told me his name—John. Her description of John exactly matched his appearance in my plant medicine journey. She confirmed our connection. I asked when we would meet, but in typical guide protocol, the answer was, "when the time is appropriate according to both of your healing journeys." This beautiful confirmation led me to fully trust in my divine path and gifts. I no longer perceive anything as coincidental.

I have had two healing sessions, in late 2022 and early 2023, with another practitioner, whose technique is a blend of energy modalities, intuition, and conscious channeling. Her sessions and conversations have been instrumental in my healing. Her methodology allows for active conversation between the two of us, in order to get to the root of issues and heal them together. This practitioner uncovered more details regarding the source of my chronic back pain, discovering that it was from a long-ago past life as a child. I had broken my back from a fall and subsequently, died a long, agonizing death. This resulted in an energetic scar, which we successfully released and healed—I literally felt the release of the energy. The chronic pain was gone, and I have had no relapse! During our second session together, the sacred mothers and their divine feminine energy came to assist with the healing and opening of my heart. With the practitioner's guidance, I energetically embraced the younger me, who had made so many mistakes and felt such shame, telling her that I loved and accepted her. I learned that self-love and forgiveness are instrumental in a healing journey.

The BQH session inspired me to travel on a spiritual, divine feminine journey throughout Egypt in November, 2023. My guides gave me three tasks: meditate in a tomb, visit the birthing house within the Temple of Isis, and find "the crystal." While visiting the catacombs in Alexandria, my intuition drew me to an isolated room. Not only did I meditate there, I was compelled to tone[1]. So much emotional pain was released! In the birthing house of the Temple of Isis, I again found myself alone. On the wall to the left of the door, I discovered my name (Kris) scratched into the wall! I placed my hands against the wall, silently meditating. I felt the Great Mother Isis, goddess of healing and magic, healing and opening my heart chakra. I found "the crystal" the last day, while visiting an alabaster shop. The shopkeeper recognized that I had an energetic connection to a particular chunk of raw alabaster and gave it to me as a gift. Within it, you can see the three pyramids of Giza. I had accomplished my mission!

---

1. Vocal toning involves emitting a tone or sound through the voice in order to assist in physical, mental, emotional, or spiritual well-being.

Later that day, at the airport, I met an Egyptian man. His first words to me were "Hello Isis, I am Horus." Our souls recognized each other instantly, and we both felt a deep love for one another. I have never felt that type of love with a man before. It was pure, divine. We sat and had a deep metaphysical conversation regarding the "old gods," love, and ascension. We held a long embrace, tears streaming down my face, when, at last, my flight was called. I meditated on this encounter during the long flight home. Initially, I thought the experience cruel but soon realized, this man was purposely placed on my path so I would know my heart was finally healed. My heart was able to feel and recognize *true love*. Recalling the message to me from my guides during the 2022 group regression / stream of consciousness session, and now, fully trusting my intuition, I have planned a trip to Scotland for December, 2024.

In addition to the experiences above, during these years of evolution, I've explored sound baths[2], a Bufo experience[3], and ecstatic dance[4]. I have participated in individual and group Reiki sessions, a galactic book study, group regression sessions, weekly meditations with my local tribe, monthly meditations with my nationwide tribe, and countless personal meditations and seminars. I've read more books than I can count. Healing was difficult initially; however, the journey has become easier with each passing day.

I am not sure if we ever heal completely, but I am sure that I am a completely different person now. I have a greater understanding of, well, everything. I know who I am and my purpose on Earth during this time of the great awakening. I recognize and rise above the

---

2. A sound bath is a "wash" of sound using intentionally curated instruments (and sometimes voice) that allow participants to release from the thought processes of the brain.

3. The Bufo alvarius toad secretes 5-MeO-DMT, a psychedelic that proponents claim can reduce anxiety, depression, and symptoms of post-traumatic stress disorder, while also providing sustained feelings of well-being.

4. Ecstatic dance allows for free movement to the music, which can stimulate dancers into a state of trance or ecstasy.

distractions, choosing to live in light and love. With that, I know I am worthy of love, happiness, and abundance. I claim it. I am.

Kristina Skirving was raised in rural Ohio. As a child, she felt a strong energetic connection to both nature and the cosmos. Depending upon the day, she wanted to be an astronaut, explorer, marine biologist, nurse, or female superhero. After holding a variety of jobs as a young adult, Kristina determined that what she wanted most was to protect and serve people. She worked as a law enforcement officer and later served twenty years in the military.

Kristina holds a Bachelor of Arts in Criminal Justice and an Associate of Applied Science in Paralegal Studies, which is her current occupation. She also holds a Usui Reiki Master teacher certification. Kristina officially opened a Reiki business, Highland Healing Hands, in November, 2022. She accepts all clients; however, Kristina's passion is working with veterans and law enforcement officers suffering from post-traumatic stress disorder, as well as cancer patients.

As Kristina's healing and ascension journey has progressed, her energy healing gifts have grown to include a heightened intuition and the ability to remove energetic scars resulting from physical and emotional trauma. She also dabbles in herbal medicine, creating tinctures, salves, and creams. Kristina has made a concerted effort to avoid chemicals and toxins entering her body. She consumes healthy foods, makes her own soaps and skin products, and has eliminated fluoride and chlorine from her water supply.

Kristina is an active solo traveler. She enjoys learning about different cultures, in tandem with enlightening metaphysical experiences. She has traveled throughout the United States, Europe, Central and South America, and Africa.

Kristina's life is blessed with peace and love. She lives each day with gratitude for herself, her family and friends, and her divine gifts.

Kristina feels the connection to Source, humanity, her galactic family, and Gaia with her every breath.

To learn more about Kris and her work, visit: https://highlandhealing hands.com/

Chapter 20
Past Lives, Reiki & Crystals, Oh My!

Christina Brady

What the H-E-double hockey sticks!!! Past lives, spirit guides, channeling, crystals, Reiki . . . surely all of these things will earn me the lowest eternal kingdom?! Maybe even outer darkness! I was taught the dangers of these things! Shouldn't I guard myself from the destruction they pose?

HA! I would never have researched even *one* of those topics, as a devout member of the high-demand religion I once belonged to: The Church of Jesus Christ of Latter-Day Saints, a.k.a. Mormon. Such activities and notions collide with the beliefs I once clung to, believed whole-heartedly to be true.

I wasn't born into religion. As a young girl, I simply wanted to understand my purpose. At the time, my child-self felt like a piece on a chess board, being moved around this game of life. I remember feeling purposeless, with no control of who was "moving" me. I yearned to be a part of something bigger, to belong, to feel supported and loved.

My younger sister and I were born and raised in central Missouri by awesome parents. They built us a home on acreage in the country and though our life wasn't always easy, we were always there for each other. Our parents came to every game and school event—I don't recall them missing anything!

Through life's ups and downs, we worked hard together, took road trips, visited extended family, and enjoyed vacations. Most every night we prioritized family meals. I'd say we were a typical, all-American, middle-class family; our parents intent on keeping life consistent and raising us the best they could. I mention this to demonstrate just how loved and supported I was. Yet, I still looked for purpose and a greater sense of belonging.

Headed into my junior year of high school, I was in a funk. I had played volleyball for the past four years but decided I really didn't want to continue on the varsity team. With no more practices, games, or special events to attend, this freed up huge amounts of time. Suddenly, my daily routine seemed bland—I went to school, took my sister home afterwards, did homework, went to work, returned home, only to start the process again the next day. I had friends but none extremely close. I dated here and there, but after a couple flings, even dating didn't feel like it was working.

Then something big happened.

My co-worker and friend, Jami, had this guy friend, and he kept begging her to get me to go out with him. I refused him several times. One night, Jami arranged for the three of us to go to the movies together. This night specifically sticks in my mind for several reasons. First of all, this guy *strategically* pulled up in a very small, cream-colored, 1984 Mazda Sundowner pickup . . . single cab, manual transmission! You know what that means, right? Yep, someone had to sit in the middle, straddling the shifter. Did I mention how small this truck was? The middle seat was double-occupied, not only by me but with the driver, who had to shift that tiny Mazda truck!

We drove to the theater, watched a romantic comedy (naturally!), titled, *Only You*, then headed back home. I believe I mentioned he was strategic—Jami's house was before mine, so we had to drop her off first. And then . . . alone at last! I don't remember moving over from the middle seat after dropping Jami off, but my curfew was still a few hours out, so we just kept driving and talking. That night I discovered my soul-mate, Dennis! A bond was forged that, from the very beginning, was unbreakable. I had met my best friend and found a piece of my purpose. From that night on, the middle seat of that little Mazda Sundowner was mine, and you wouldn't find one of us without the other!

This teenage part of my story is essential. You see, Dennis was a Mormon. And much of my awakening journey began with him. As most members of the Mormon church can tell you, the goal for any eighteen-year-old son is sending him on a two-year service mission to share the gospel of Christ with the world. Dennis was encouraged by his family and church friends to drop me like a bad habit! His family went so far as to move him to Arizona with the hope that we would forget about each other, freeing him up for his "calling."

This did not work. They truly didn't understand the bond we had!

Dennis must have learned strategy from his family, because their next step was, "convert the girl." Why? Their beliefs dictated that to make it to the highest kingdom in the afterlife, you must seal yourself to your family for eternity in the temple. This applies only to Mormons because it's believed only Mormons will be in the Celestial Kingdom. So for us to have any life or future together, I needed to become a Mormon.

Really, it wasn't at all difficult for me to join. Mormons believe in "pre-mortal life"—the concept of living in heaven, together, as a large family before coming to this earth; further, that our older brother Jesus Christ agreed to come to Earth to die for us, so we could live in

Heaven again. As a child who had yearned for a purpose, to belong and feel deeply supported, I was now being presented with the

Love of my life AND the deeper things I'd sought, in one magnificent, tidy package! *Of course,* I not only joined their church but became a dedicated member of it!

I checked all the boxes, sealed in the temple for eternity, raised four children with Mormon beliefs, and sent our kids on missions for the church. We were *all in*! We gave ten percent of our income. We served in callings, gave freely of our time and resources. We raised our children with strong standards, which helped us through a lot of life's challenges. But as our children started leaving the house to marry, another major shift began.

Our four children are very close in age, so shortly after one started dating, they were *all* dating—subsequently, they were all married within a thirteen-month span! Alongside that, COVID-19 happened. In the broader world, questions were arising about many topics, belief systems included . . . disclosure started happening. Timing, of course, is everything.

Dennis had never swallowed all the church's teachings. "Policy and Politics!" is the phrase he often used. When he came across *CES Letter: My Search for Answers to my Mormon Doubts*, by Jeremy T. Runnells, and shared it with me, my world started to unravel. Usually, if something challenged my religious beliefs, I just ignored it or pushed it aside. Yet, for some reason, I agreed to entertain this text, quite confident that nothing would change my strong beliefs. Boy, was I wrong! Dennis and I read it together, sometimes through tears, anger, and even disgust. We learned the truth of the Mormon church: its history, its foundation, and its holy book, *The Book of Mormon*. The impact was huge. Everything in the letter was backed by references; this was critical for me, because even as we read, I was looking for a way to disagree with it. That experience was, perhaps, the fulcrum of my "awakening," the major inner shift.

I had always loved being right . . . being in control . . . knowing the *truth*. (My poor ego, right?!) I preached about "truth" for twenty-six years. Truth is *foundational* for members of the church—but for the first time in twenty-six years of unquestioning belief, I realized that the Mormon truth was no longer *my* truth! I felt ridiculously naïve, ashamed of how I had tried to convince people that I had the truth that they needed. What I understand, now, is that we all have different truths that we live by—it's a beautiful part of this earthly life, a beauty I personally hold dear!

But in the meantime, life as I had known it was shattered! That's a pretty strong word, but that is truly how I felt: SHATTERED. I had given every ounce of every waking moment to being a good Mormon, and suddenly, I didn't know what my truth even was or how to find it. I was scared, confused, angry . . . my emotions pretty much ran the gamut. I was trying to rediscover purpose and security all over again.

If the church wasn't where truth was found, then where could I turn?

Eventually, Dennis and I sat our kids (and their spouses) down, to explain that we were exiting the church, feeling it no longer aligned with us. We encouraged them to live however they felt would best serve them. We simply asked that they "love us at our level" and not judge us, giving us the freedom to learn and grow in the way that we felt was best for us. There were many tears.

Our leaving meant that we would miss our oldest daughter's most important life event: She and her husband were to be sealed for eternity in the temple soon . . . one of those life events I had preached the importance of since they were little. As you can imagine, I was still feeling shattered! Thankfully, our children are awesome humans. As hard as this was for everyone, they gave us the space and love to follow what we felt was important. They know us deeply enough to understand that we wouldn't make a choice like this lightly.

Now what? Rock bottom only has one direction—up! So how to find my way back up from this bottom? With Dennis' support, one breath at a time, one day at a time, I slowly began. As weeks and months passed, I recognized even deeper layers of religious programming. I'd find myself adjusting my thoughts, giving myself permission to just be, freeing myself to think and feel differently.

Doors began to open and a new journey launched!

One day, while visiting Dennis' sister, she shared a personal experience in which she'd learned about a past life and revisited it. Umm, a past life? At this point, I was trying to be open-minded—all my previous beliefs having been shattered—so why not? She mentioned Dolores Cannon, a self-trained hypnotherapist. Dennis reminded me that he had mentioned Dolores to me years ago, something I didn't recall, probably because I simply dismissed it at the time. As we traveled home, I purchased Dolores' audio books on Jesus. I gorged on those books, trying to discover who Jesus really was. I thought, if I could find a person who has had a past life with Jesus, I could get some answers, maybe find the *real* truth!

While working out my own (new) beliefs and purpose, the idea of past lives intrigued me. So many possibilities might open up if could I help people like Dolores Cannon did, not to mention what I'd learn about my own journey. So I began to dig for scripts and guided meditations. I searched the internet, searched for and purchased books, and listened to YouTube videos. Dolores' course popped up, and I wondered, *should I purchase it?* I didn't know Dolores' whole story, yet I couldn't stop thinking about how she had created her own way of learning and practicing. Surely, if she did it, I—a true DIYer— could too. I looked up local hypnosis practitioners and even called one, but it didn't seem like a good fit. Instead, I searched Dolores' Quantum Healing Hypnosis Therapy (QHHT®) directory for local practitioners who were trained in her method. There were a couple with level one experience, but I wasn't sure a level one would know enough to help me.

Finally, I discovered Candace Craw-Goldman, who had known, been taught by, and become an assistant to Dolores Cannon. Candace created the Beyond Quantum Healing modality, also known as BQH. After discussion with Dennis, I jumped on board and took the online BQH course, during which, I discovered Candace's in-person Immersion class. I rushed through the BQH course (a prerequisite for the immersion) so I could sign up for the week-long, in-person experience. It started to sink in: *I was going to meet Candace Craw-Goldman!* For reasons that weren't clear at the time, simply meeting Candace felt as significant as learning from her. In the meantime, I needed some practice sessions . . . and fast!

Family members were first, and I'm grateful for those who were open to being practiced on! Dennis was a champ—I took him on the first journey, during which he visited a past life scene as a knight. My sister-in-law, who had introduced me to past lives, got roped in too. These sessions were exciting, and I was thrilled to finally be practicing . . . yet I still felt unprepared for the immersion class.

Driving home one day, a simple sign on the curb caught my attention: *Metaphysical.* Okay, I thought to myself, I'll go see what it is. I turned around, pulled into the parking lot, and took a deep breath, reminding myself that this was allowed. I stepped inside, casually perusing tables of crystals. Skipping past the crystal penises, blushing . . . (*what are those used for?* I wondered), I meandered over to the magic wands and all manner of "witchy" looking stuff. By then my heart was pounding. The shop attendant was busy with a customer, so I retreated back to my car, thinking, *Ugh, maybe this isn't for me!*

Continuing to study was easy. Finding people to practice on was not. Most of my friends were members of a religion who would frown mightily upon this. I passed the metaphysical shop a few more times before stopping in again. By plucking up the courage to talk to the person at the counter and share what I was learning, I hoped to find someone or something to help me. Walking in, I made a beeline to the counter—*drop the programing, drop the programing*—avoiding the crystal penises and witchy corner. A woman poked her head up, greeting me kindly, and my nervous system relaxed a bit. Speaking quickly so as not to lose my momentum, I told her I was taking an online course for past life regressions.

"Who is your teacher?" she asked.

"Candace Craw-Goldman."

And just like that, she shared that Candace was a personal friend of hers! The shop owner, Samantha—a channeler, herself—understood this new "language." To my surprise, she even volunteered for a practice session with me. One Saturday, Samantha allowed me to come to the shop to share my name and what I do, with her customers. During that meet-and-greet, I met a Reiki Practitioner who announced that she, too, was taking the online BQH course! I was shocked and excited to find someone else who might want to practice together. *Thank you, Universe, for your guidance!*

Since that day, I joined the Quantum Healers forum—a large community of spiritual and metaphysical practitioners—and now have a huge network of practitioners to chat with about my sessions and experiences. Reading *The Journey Within*, by Dr. Allison Brown —also a forum member—helped me connect the dots between spirituality and religion. An in-person retreat with Allison and her husband, Will, further accelerated my awakening; Dennis attended with me, as he, too, is on his own journey. Together, we enjoyed a full day of yoga, meditation, and sound baths, and even created our own selenite wand. Ha! It's so funny to think back on how different this was for us . . . seriously . . . we crafted selenite wands!? We've both expanded a lot since that trip.

Throughout this process, I continue to meet amazing people, building a new tribe as we research, practice, and play with all the energetics. New connections have been essential to my growth and helping me move forward. I've taken a Reiki course from the local Reiki teacher I met and received a delightful channeling from Samantha-the-purveyor-of-crystal-penises-and-witchy-things, at her crystal shop. Dennis and I have had several BQH sessions together. Each time, we come to understand more and more about the deeper meanings and purposes in life. I've learned how to facilitate tandem sessions (in which two people "go under" together) and group hypnotic regression sessions.

Pondering this *awakening* story, I realize it's a continuing journey for me, rather than one major moment. Each day brings new discoveries; some are large and some are small. A recent one is learning to channel—to process energy through my body, in my case, verbally. I was invited by a friend to channel Jesus after asking her a question about the biblical story the "Garden of Gethsemane." She casually mentioned we could channel Jesus and ask him directly. Things like this still stir that religious programming within, and I am reminded to give myself permission to explore and feel worthy of all things. Once I thought about it, channeling seemed similar to communicating in prayer—you just strengthen that connection by being in a relaxed state.

Every event in my life has led to who and where I am today; I wouldn't change any of it. Each moment, choice, and new acquaintance has become a beautiful piece in the larger picture of my personal journey, a journey that indeed continues.

Christina Brady is an experienced stay-at-home mom, educator, and quantum healer. In 2021 during the disclosure that begin to show up for humanity, Christina found herself in a shift of her own as she discovered that her high demand religion no longer aligned.

Leaving the Church of Jesus Christ of Latter-Day Saints, a.k.a Mormonism, Christina's world opened up to a completely new reality. Christina began the path of rediscovering who she really is and where she came from, giving herself permission to explore spirituality in greater depth. Even though she is no longer a member of the church, she realizes that her years of experience gifted her with an understanding of those in and outside of religion, as well as the ability to love others at their own level.

After her exodus from the Mormon religion, Christina discovered Dolores Cannon, which sparked an interest in uncovering her own past life connections. Christina, enjoying this journey, went on to become a Quantum Healing Practitioner by certifying in Candace Craw-Goldman's online Beyond Quantum Healing and Quantum Connect courses, as well as some Reiki courses. Using these modalities, she now facilitates quantum healing sessions to assist others through transition and self-healing in their own lives.

Family is important to Christina. Married to her husband since 1995, they have four amazing children. Her family grew, and they all, now, have spouses of their own. Being "Mimi" to her grandchildren has added the cherry on the top of life.

With much life to live and more adventures to attend to, this beautiful path will continue to unfold.

To find out more about Christina visit www.ConsciousnessConnectionsWithCB.com

Contact Christina via email at connectionwithcb@gmail.com

Chapter 21
A Kaleidoscope of Awakenings
Mona Thiel

It has been my experience that an "Awakening" is not an event but a multi-layered kaleidoscope of evolutionary thresholds and transformative shifts of consciousness. There have been multiple "awakenings" in my life leading to my present state of Awakening. Each one was *divinely summoned* by that still, small light, which became an actualized beacon of rebirthing and expansion.

For as long as I could remember, I never felt like I fit in. I felt I was never enough, when compared to the "norms" of society and those around me. I seemed to view the world through different lenses and "outside the box" from a very small age; reality didn't make sense to me in many ways. Though I was raised by and within a beautiful loving family, blessed by many opportunities to feel the richness of life, while being provided guidance to strive for greater heights, my small town in Kansas began to feel way too small, as my consciousness expanded beyond what I thought was the true essence of life. As much as I tried to fit in, what satisfied many people, as a way of life, didn't quench my passion for more worldly things. I remember laying in the front yard, around age ten, in hopes that "the mothership" was going to land; I felt no fear, only anticipation. I was in search of truth, whatever that was—answers to my multitude of questions regarding a higher experience of life, love, and more importantly, God—that just wasn't being quenched. My "not enough-ness" began calling out for people, places, things and eventually, mind-altering substances, to fill the caverns of my heart that felt empty.

As I graduated from high school in 1970, the social revolution had made its way into the Midwest. I knew I wanted to go out and experience the world beyond the womb of my hometown, instead of following the typical path—in alignment with the vision of my parents and society—of going to college, settling down, and raising a family. I tried the college scene for a year, and I just didn't vibe with taking courses that I felt I would never use, not to mention that it didn't fill my soul's calling. I was led to work in the field of developmental disabilities, as a summer research assistant at our local hospital and research center and then on to more full-time work for the next year. It was now 1972 and my "hippie," free-spirited energy began kicking in, along with all the possibilities! I asked the doctor I worked for to support me in relocating somewhere in the field of developmental disabilities. My heart sang with a newfound purpose when I connected with an angel in Nashville, Tennessee, who saw my light and offered me a job as a behavioral assistant in a large state-run institution. With hesitancy and great concern, my parents supported my sojourn to Nashville at the age of nineteen; I believe they thought it would not last long. I never returned.

I was always a "bleeding heart" when it came to people and animals who seemed less advantaged than me, and I had grown up always wanting to help others (another gift of my upbringing). As I drove into the gates of Clover Bottom Hospital for the Feebleminded, as it was called in 1972, my body shuddered in an eerie premonition of what was to come and my divinely-appointed purpose for being here. Intellectually, and at a very deep soul level, I felt in complete alignment and rose with passion to work at this institution, serving those with developmental disabilities. However, my heart and my spirit were unsure, emotionally, that I would have the courage to withstand what I suspected would be my role.

Fortunately, there were others who were part of my *spiritual team*, as well as other free spirits, like myself, ready to "suit up and show up," to offer the hospital residents independence and empowerment— more of a voice—while cautiously abiding within the structures rigidly put in place. We endeavored to make only enough waves to accomplish the mission without being terminated or viewed as a threat. So many times, I just had to surf the waves and serve with the motto that, "It's easier to ask for forgiveness than for permission." As I look back and remember the individuals I served in the beginning of my career, I'm filled with gratitude for all they taught me about connecting with another human being soul-to-soul, rather than their physicality or their survival behaviors.

This small-town girl quickly *awaken*ed to life in "the big city," with many ups and downs after growing up in a town of fourteen-thousand people. The feeling of being alone and small really felt scary at times, but my gift of connecting with others was my saving grace. I loved the new adventures, interesting people, and the nightlife— letting my uninhibited Self spread her wings with the aid of alcohol. I worked hard and played hard in the excitement of Music City. As I look back, when my experiences at work felt too emotionally heavy, I see now, that this was a cunning way of balancing for the very important mission I was sent there for.

In 1975, the Individuals with Disabilities Education Act was passed, which led to a huge movement to deinstitutionalize many residents into community-based group homes; I was off and running! I connected with a community-based group home agency and became a house manager for a group home in Nashville, just off music row, housing eight developmentally-disabled adults. *It was an awakening I was not anticipating.* These powerful and courageous people entered a foreign world but one with opportunities, challenges, and empowering transformations. It was an unforgettable experience!

Being a bridge for them into a community and world that, for the most part, was not ready to receive them was monumental, and I grew in innumerable ways. While in Nashville through the late '70s, advocating for those with disabilities was my calling but so was my party life, and it was starting to take a toll on me. I would hear that small but piercing voice insisting, *you're an alcoholic . . . you're an alcoholic*. It shouted through deaf ears, however, because I was in denial . . . .and in fear that if I gave up alcohol, I would lose one of my "best friends" and myself.

In 1980 as I continued to search for that *something* outside myself that could fill the void in my heart and heal my spiritual brokenness, I was divinely led by a friend and colleague to the Institute for Self-Actualization (ISA). This was my first intensive exposure to the truth of who I was—uncovering my woundedness and putting me on a path to joyful reconnection, rebirthing, and awakening to my authentic beingness. I immersed myself within a community where I felt I belonged, and in the course of two years, peeled off layers upon layers of beliefs and conditionings that no longer defined me. I faced the pain I had created from my self-abandonment and denial and was given the tools, resources, and energetic, loving connections to fill up those empty caverns in my heart. *A powerful awakening*.

By 1981, after experiencing a state of renewal and broadened horizons, my restlessness started rising again after meeting a man with like-energy—Florida was our new destination. A flatbed truck loaded down with all of our belongings headed for new adventures! What I didn't know, and was not prepared for on a conscious level, was that this new and exciting adventure would ultimately lead to the greatest timeline shift in my life.

After arriving in Florida within this new relationship with a man— and myself—I realized that, with "beach life," came a whole new mesmerizing world of people in search of an illusion "outside the box" on so many levels. Being raised in Kansas hadn't offered me an ocean experience until I was twenty-one, so I spent the first year hanging out on the beach with the seductive allure of alcohol, the world of scuba diving, and with other souls searching for the fantasy life in paradise. I soon realized that my relationship with alcohol and security was stronger than with my new partner, so we went our separate ways. But in that pregnant void, I realized it was time to re-establish *professional* Mona.

I entered a new job serving twenty-four human beings with developmental disabilities and supervising forty to fifty direct care staff members. Through those first years, I was blessed with beautiful mentorship by those I worked for and gained much expansion and many creative opportunities in educating the community about developmental disabilities. Again, I worked hard, always taking on more community leadership roles, while managing a very stressful work environment. But I also played hard . . . still relying on my old friend, Alcohol, to be my guide, my best friend, and even my God, in extreme situations . . . always subduing my loneliness within an ongoing estrangement that was occurring between me and my Soul at an increasingly rapid pace. I was burning out in mind, body, and spirit, and the walls were closing in . . . .

I spent a major amount of time and energy concealing what I knew deep inside: I was an alcoholic. There came a point when I could no longer hold the dam of denial, guilt, shame, and self-loathing from those around me. The Universe finally stepped in—thank God—the afternoon that my car collided with a minister's, one block from my home after a pool party. I arrived at the emergency room with a state trooper next to me, questioning all the empty beer cans in brown bags that had flown out of my vehicle upon impact. Somehow, by the grace of God, I did not get a DUI—the Minister was instrumental in my clarity and self-forgiveness—a true miracle . . . .and another awakening. Two days later, my supervisor, who was a dear friend (and an angel), gave me an ultimatum: surrender my alcoholism and go to Alcoholics Anonymous (AA) or lose my job. Broken and surrendered, I called a therapist friend that very morning, requesting that she go with me to an AA meeting, for what would turn out to be the grand *awakening* of a new chapter of my life on March 8th, 1992.

I never turned back; it had taken me soooo damned long to surrender.

The next year was surreal. I felt like I had been plucked from one identity into a rebirthed version of myself that was so foreign and that I had long forgotten . . . .and in some realms, was meeting for the first time. It was the most humbly vulnerable and surrendered time in my life, as I overcame the humiliation of being demoted. I was demoted in my job status to facilitate less responsibility and stress, viewed with less authority and leadership capability, treated with less respect, and perceived to require more supervision. I was perched upon a questionable threshold of where I was headed next . . . until the *awakening* jolted me again.

Over the following two years, as I went to many AA meetings a week, surrounded myself with friends in recovery and a wonderful recovery sponsor, worked through the recovery steps with zeal, and sponsored others, I discovered that my heart of gold, my giving spirit, and my shiny soul became even more illumined than ever before. I was like a phoenix rising from the ashes. Thanks to God!!

I became more and more aligned with who I was becoming, purely and organically, with a sense of divinity I had never known. I was like a sponge, soaking in all that I could learn, be, and share. For the first time in my life, I drew on my own source of love, strength, wisdom, and inner security, instead of looking for a man or a substance outside of myself to fill in the missing colors of my heart. I spent three years "nesting" within this beautiful new womb, as I re-entered an expansive horizon of self-honoring love, rebuilding relationships with family and friends, and making conscious choices from a place of wholeness instead of mere survival, lack, or "looking for love in all the wrong places." To this day, gratitude is my mantra, and I know in my heart of hearts, it saved my life.

Fast forward seven years later . . . I met a strong and spirited man who was a guide for me in so many ways. I sensed this relationship was part of the new, healthier me, and in some ways, proving to my parents that I could settle down. We shared a zest for life and adventure, married in 2000, and relocated from Florida to Maryland for his work and for what I would discover was another chapter of my life and many new *awakenings*. The seeds were planted for yet another important awakening of my journey and for the harvest of greater revelations of the authenticity and wholeness of who I am today.

I had never had the luxury of not working, until my life began to unfold in Maryland in a charming Victorian community that held much kindred-ship for me, almost like a past life connection. I embraced it with passion and began to feel at home in my heart more and more. It was during this time that I became a Reiki Master, and through this spiritual journey, longed for more inner discoveries and answers to even more questions regarding my purpose and the calling of my soul.

In 2008 I entered the Inner Vision Institute for Spiritual Development, with the intention of becoming a Spiritual Life Coach and learning all that I would need to know to help others. I had the honor of studying with Rev. Dr. Iyanla VanZant, herself, the founder of the worldwide institute. Little did I know, it would be the most intensive two years of humbling self-discovery, rigorous honesty, and heart-full integration, realization, and alignment of God within me I had ever experienced. I was held accountable in some heartfully deep ways by those who loved me enough to support my healing and reflect the truth of who I was. I was brought to my knees, as I surrendered my resistance and those core beliefs that had calcified me, revealing new layers of healing in areas I thought had been healed. I experienced the healing of important relationships beginning with ME. As a result, I was lifted and empowered to comprehend the immense amount of love I truly was and could offer to the world in ways that I had previously viewed as unworthy and unattainable. Through that time, I expanded my ability to receive love, beginning with fully loving and honoring myself. I rebirthed and *awakened* to an authentic version of myself that I had never known, which also led to the ending of my marriage and the spirited, divinely guided horizons of today.

My present awakening is the miracle of living in the now, within a beautiful healing sanctuary that cradled me so tenderly after my divorce in 2011. My dear friend, who owns this magical place opened her heart and her home to me, at that time, as I healed and rebirthed in one of the most raw and vulnerable times of my life. The tiny dwelling below her cottage taught me to breathe in the true essence of life through the peace, love, and heart-full presence of Mother Earth right outside my door, as I surrendered to my soul's callings and enjoyed sacred time with myself.

In 2013 I met a man who I was ready to open my heart to. After one year, I realized I had chosen someone who supported my healing and in turn, brought me to completion. I was no longer willing to abandon myself just to experience the illusion of a "loving" connection. We became better friends than lovers, and we remained friends until his death.

In 2021, as I began searching for a new place to live, away from the bustle of town, I called my dear friend to join me in prayerful visioning and learned that she was "coincidentally" planning to meet with a management company the next day to rent the sanctuary, as she was getting married and moving. We knew, in that powerful moment, that "divine providence" had occurred! Needless to say, I am back in my beautiful, heart-full sanctuary, living in a cozy light-filled cottage that holds women's retreats, sound healings, and a multitude of gatherings, while offering much balanced sovereign time for myself. My adjacent studio brings forward healing opportunities for others through individual sessions, Reiki classes, and whatever else flows through. I am guided in an organic, spirited flow, to offer healing opportunities for all who are drawn to this magical place.

I know in my heart of hearts that each *awakening* on my path was spiritually cultivated in order to be readied for the next—a true kaleidoscope—as each colorful experience of my journey has offered me a spectrum of heart prints to live by. I now know that my feeling of "not enough-ness" simply meant that my soul contract here was and is uniquely different than those around me, by divine design. I rise with loving and self-trusting, sovereign alignment. And the journey continues . . . .

Mona Thiel is a Spirited Sojourner, a Truth Seeker, and an Energy Alchemist in this journey called life. The humble intention of her healing offerings serves as a bridge to heart-full awakening as an Usui Holy Fire Master Reiki practitioner/teacher, Certified Medical Reiki Master, Certified Reflexologist, and Spiritual Coach.

Mona entered the journey of wholistic healing after serving people with developmental disabilities for over twenty-eight years in a continuum of services. She has been practicing and teaching Reiki for over twenty years and practicing reflexology for eight years.

She is a graduate of the Inner Visions Institute for Spiritual Development Program, studying under nationally acclaimed author and Spiritual Coach Rev. Dr. Iyanla Vanzant, as well as a graduate of the International Institute of Reflexology. Mona studied medical Reiki under Medical Reiki Master, Raven Keyes.

Her passion in serving others is within a focus of self-honoring love, empowerment, and life visioning. To that end, Mona provides and teaches Reiki, Energy Healing and Reflexology, group retreats, workshops, and other processes, in order to release self-imposed barriers to love, light and joy. It is Mona's powerful intention to consistently heal within to demonstrate, be on-purpose, and facilitate others to share the message of love and wholistic life fulfillment.

Visit Mona's website: www.MonathielReikimasterteacher.com

Contact her at: Mfrespearit@aol.com

Chapter 22
Becoming Galactic
Harry Kroner, MS

Boom!

The first thing I felt was the excruciating pain from the seat belt and the airbag deploying. My knee was throbbing insistently, as well. I realized, in that moment, I had crashed my car! It happened in a fraction of a second; I had fallen asleep at the wheel and smashed into a light post.

I was exhausted, jet lagged, and it was one in the morning after a long day at work. My first thoughts were, *Thank god I'm okay and no one is hurt!* I wouldn't be able to forgive myself if I had been seriously injured, or worse, dead. My wife and kids didn't deserve that; I love them too much. A quick self-assessment informed me that my injuries weren't terrible, so I climbed out of the vehicle, realizing it was totaled. At that moment, a clear message from deep within popped into my head:

If I continue on this path, I will either die, physically, or will have suffered a death of the soul—having sold out to the chase of climbing up the corporate ladder for a job I didn't really love. This cannot be what my life is all about.

It was time to change course!

The Road to Awakening

Allow me to go back a few years. My awakening story began in my early twenties. I had recently finished my military service in intelligence, where I had also met the love of my life. It was time to begin our life together. Starting out in a new place, where nobody knows you, can be challenging, and although I learned a lot from my military experience, it was difficult to translate those skills to the civilian world.

While I was busy with simple jobs, trying to get my bearings in life, I enjoyed deep conversations with my parents and my wife on topics ranging from world events, history, philosophy, and the meaning of life. We stumbled upon some spiritual books, and in spite of my skeptical nature to things not "proven," they struck a deep chord within me.

This was three decades ago, before the internet existed. The only source of information in the area of awakening was in the tiny Metaphysics/New Age/Spirituality section of my local bookstore or library.

I read books like, *Many Lives, Many Masters* by Brian Weiss, and *Journey of Souls* by Michael Newton. The world and what lay beyond started making sense to me. I had a very secular upbringing, and I didn't resonate with how limiting organized religions were. Non-religious explanations of the world and our existence were difficult for me to obtain. Through these books, I finally found a way to be spiritual without the accompanying baggage. Once I acquired that balance within me, I realized that it had been missing my entire young life. This purer explanation of the mysteries of life really felt as if the truth had finally been revealed to me.

During that period, I switched from a being a non-believer to believing in the soul and our eternal nature as Beings. Early on, there were many gaps in my understanding, not to mention that these concepts weren't necessarily applicable to "regular" life at that time; but the switch had been created. Learning about deeper concepts such as reincarnation and the differences between the soul, oversoul, and soul groups, suddenly became my way of seeing the world.

I turned into a book worm, reading anything I could put my hands on in the metaphysical and spiritual realm—books by Deepak Chopra, Bruce Goldberg, Ram Dass, Wayne Dyer, Neale Donald Walsch, Jon Kabat-Zin—absorbing a great deal of knowledge and wisdom. Admittedly, these concepts were hard to digest and absorb, at first. I could feel how my world scheme was challenged; it needed to adjust and get reconstructed in a new way.

In my new fascination, I noticed that all of my favorite works about past lives, reincarnation, and soul work had a common method—*hypnosis*. This is the key to unlocking our consciousness, and I was excited to learn more about it! Initially, I trained in hypnosis for the purpose of exploring the vastness of consciousness. The first course I enrolled in was quite basic, but it was fun to learn along with my wife and mom, who were curious about it, as well. At the time, I had a dream of doing this for a living, although it seemed far-fetched and unattainable—nevertheless, the seed had been sown.

In the beginning, we practiced hypnosis sessions within the family, exploring past lives and age regressions, and tapping into high levels of consciousness. It was all extremely exciting, but we felt we had to keep it very hush hush. Being a closeted spiritual person was challenging, but back then, it was very rare to find people to talk to about these topics.

These experiences opened my consciousness wide, and I started having vivid dreams, out of body experiences, and premonitions. Back then, I didn't have the words to describe what was happening, but in hindsight, I can easily recognize that it was my awakening to psychic gifts, intuition, and other abilities that had laid dormant for many years.

My dream and strong pull to work in hypnotherapy was powerful, yet I did not feel ready to assist people without broader knowledge. I needed conventional learning tools to solidify my education and credentials, so I decided to go to college to study psychology. It was not easy to work full time and study full time. However, I deeply enjoyed exploring concepts on a higher level. The educational environment itself was enriching—through that experience, I truly learned a lot more about people, the world, and myself.

Our family was growing, so I changed direction, taking a promotion at work, into a management role. Work was hard, with many long hours. I had almost no time to dedicate to my studies or reading books. I stepped away from the spiritual path, with only glimpses of it remaining in my life. I was constantly pushed to work harder and climb the managerial levels. I felt empty inside; years went by, and I was getting further and further away from my true Self.

And then . . . the accident happened. I knew I needed to pivot my life, acting with deliberate intention. With the endless support of my wife, who believed in me more than I believed in myself, I quit my job. I compromised, taking on what seemed to be an easier managerial job that offered me more flexibility to enroll in evening college courses. Another four painful years went by. I finally finished the last class of my bachelor's degree in psychology, but I was also dealing with a new boss that I really did not get along with. I knew it was time to go. My wife and I figured out a plan, whereby I could work a part-time job, while completing a master's degree in psychology.

The universe had provided me with a pivotal opportunity, and I took the leap, leaving a secure income, ready to plunge into the next phase in my life . . . into the unknown. It was risky, considering my mortgage and two young children, but I realized if I didn't try, I would be miserable forever.

Stepping into My Mission and Purpose

I always erred on the side of *conventional* rather than *alternative*. Although I had been accepted into the master's program, deep inside, I knew that what I really wanted to do was the deeper spiritual work. I started to reconsider my decision to spend three more years in school. I had a burning desire to help people *now*, in a different way, and I was feeling more and more aligned with my mission and purpose. I decided to postpone the master's degree, (eventually completing it several years later), and started educating myself. I took more hypnosis classes and studied deep healing methods, life coaching, Neuro-linguistic Programming (NLP), and energy healing. I read a stupendous number of books on relevant topics. There was deep excitement within; I knew I was tapping into the work of my life. I had clear vision and a dream around what I wanted to create—visualizing an abundance of clients—and I felt deeply fortunate to be able to do this work.

I secured a small office in town, completing all of the necessary task related to opening a business. I was excited and very driven but also full of self-doubt about my skills and abilities, wondering whether I could really pull it off and make a decent living. The financial dread loomed over me, yet I knew that I was engaged in the most rewarding and thrilling pursuit of my life.

Three years after I started my practice, I was finally able to let go of the part-time job I still held, in order to dedicate myself fully to my craft. This felt exceptionally rewarding, and I was thrilled with my work as a facilitator of deep healing for those dealing with trauma, strained relationships, unresolved emotions, fears, and phobias. I was helping people discover their mission and purpose in life, and so much more. In addition, I continued to learn a great deal from my clients, thus growing exponentially in my skills and gifts. I also discovered how to heal myself through this work. That being said, in some areas I felt like a shoeless shoemaker. As I was helping everyone else connect with higher guidance from their spirit guides, Higher Self, and divine Beings, I had a hard time connecting to my own.

Self-Mastery

One day, while working with a friend who was a skillful channeler, we were exploring, asking questions of his spirit guides. I asked them why I couldn't channel *my* spirit guides? Why did I not have that ability? They laughed, and said, "Of course you can; everyone can. You just need to *know* that you can, and start practicing."

This rattled my belief system . . . and yet . . . was extremely liberating!

I started guiding myself into journeys (meditations) to connect with my spirit guides. At first the connection was choppy and not always strong, but they encouraged me to continue, to develop this skill and build a relationship with them. They provided me with tools and techniques to work more proficiently with my clients, connecting with them more efficiently. They also helped me solve challenges in all areas of my own life. It took me a while to develop trust and to believe in what I was receiving, but the communication with my guides proved itself reliable again and again. My life was gradually getting better and better with their constant guidance.

Over the next few years, I learned how to connect with many more Beings that have my highest good in mind, and I started channeling their words of wisdom through me. They helped me tremendously in writing my book, *Freedom from Anxiety: A Deeper Approach to Healing.* The gap between my human Self and soul level consciousness was shrinking. Even now, I connect with them daily—they assist me in cultivating the right approach towards people, life, and myself. The guides are also imbuing me with new healing methods and better techniques to apply towards my clients, as well as to teach my students.

Becoming Galactic

Twelve years ago, I studied Quantum Healing Hypnosis Technique (QHHT®) with Dolores Cannon, which opened me to a whole new level of work, along with the concepts that *everything* has consciousness and our souls don't just incarnate on Earth but on other planets, as well.

My first encounter with a galactic Being was through a client of mine who was experiencing a past life in the jungles of South America, and she was preparing to connect with her "star brothers and sisters." My curiosity piqued, I intuitively asked if I could speak to one of those Beings. My client started a series of breaths and began shimmering—I could see tiny energy waves dancing across her body—as she raised her vibration in preparation for communication. The next thing I knew, my client began speaking in a completely different tone, bringing forth beautiful, healing messages. These Beings had a deep message for humanity, as well, regarding how humans can progress on their spiritual journeys. In that moment, I was awestruck . . . speaking to such an advanced Being that had our highest good in mind. What a gift!

Very quickly, this became the norm in my sessions—I had the privilege of connecting with many highly evolved Beings that delivered deep healing and guidance to my clients. The ease in which my clients connected with them astonished me. I noticed common themes, healing, and wisdom being shared with so many from the soul level—a journey that is infinite, through different dimensions, universes, and simultaneous levels of existence. I realized that I was literally being taught—by galactic masters from a higher dimension—about the nature of reality.

Throughout the years of connecting with and learning from my guides, light councils, and other highly evolved Beings, they always referred to me as *brother*, telling me that I was one of them. At first, I was puzzled . . . I felt so small and insignificant compared to them. I asked many questions, and they helped me understand that we all experience different lives in other civilizations across the universe. They explained that I was an emissary or ambassador, of sorts—in another dimension I am their equal—currently on a mission to Earth to learn, grow, and teach. This concept was difficult to absorb . . . it would take a deeper experience to truly embody this.

One evening, after a very activating, energy healing course I had hosted in my center, I went home and felt a strong urge to step outside and look at the stars. I was connecting with galactic Beings; they told me to look at Aldebaran (a red, giant star in the constellation Taurus) and said, "You have lived in many civilizations across the universe but this was your first one." In an instant, a deep recognition hit me, my whole body shuddered, and I found myself sobbing uncontrollably. Throughout my entire life, I felt something was missing, a certain longing to a distant home, a sadness that was always in the background. Now, in a flash, that feeling uplifted and cleared away. This recognition of my true nature and origin was a revelation, a deep truth that can never be taken away. I was, in that moment, seeing my own galactic nature in the most intimate and beautiful way. The inner conflict of being both a starseed and a human has been released, and I have been able to truly embrace my entire being with clarity and deep inner peace.

In the following years, I continued to refine myself and grow. I embraced my role as a galactic spiritual teacher and a facilitator of the evocation of consciousness, to help others heal, grow, and open to their true, expanded Self . . . careful to make sure the ego and spiritual ego do not interfere with the pure work and teachings. My offerings have expanded from one-on-one client sessions to more classes and workshops.

A very gifted colleague and I started facilitating a local starseed group —truly breaking ground in the depth of the expansive galactic work we were introducing. I developed a beautiful relationship with one particular galactic guide that was helping me, during the guided experiences, to verbalize what the participants needed, in the moment, to activate them in a bigger way.

My guides encouraged me to create and start teaching a comprehensive modality that I call Quantum Healing Methods™. They instruct me on what course to teach next and what to focus on for the highest good of humanity's ascension. It is the most rewarding experience imaginable, to show others what they are capable of! We truly are powerful, eternal Beings in the midst of a great spiritual awakening.

My awakening path was long and is still evolving. In spite of the immense struggles of choosing a harder path, it is the path my soul chose to experience in this lifetime. I am now more peaceful, clear, wise, and empowered than I have ever been.

Awakening is an infinite process of ascension back to Source. It is now *your* time . . . to evoke your next leap in consciousness, becoming an empowered and healed version of yourself that is fulfilling your soul's mission and purpose on this earth. Whatever that mission is, it is your destiny. Embrace it!

Harry Kroner is an author, teacher, healer, and founder of Infinite Ascension Academy. Holding a master's degree in psychology and over twenty years of experience, he has been trained extensively in hypnotherapy, past life regression, spirit guide connection, soul coaching, galactic expansion and healing, energy healing, breathwork, Quantum Healing Hypnosis Technique®, and Beyond Quantum Healing.

Harry is the author of the book, *Freedom from Anxiety: A Deeper Approach to Healing,* as well as co-author of *The Change 3: Insights into Self-Empowerment,* with Jim Lutes and Jim Britt.

Harry developed the modality, Quantum Healing Methods™, a comprehensive body of work that encompasses all of his studies, experience, and insight, designed to help others reach deep healing, self-mastery, spiritual awakening, and galactic expansion. He now certifies practitioners all over the world to facilitate this type of deep and life changing work through his online program.

Harry has helped thousands of people access the higher dimensions of themselves, reach wisdom, and experience emotional healing, while also finding their purpose and learning lessons from this life and other lives. He continues to work one-on-one with people, either in person or online, while also teaching courses through the online academy he founded.

Learn more about Harry Kroner:

https://www.harrykroner.com/

Check out courses & workshops online:

https://www.infiniteascensionacademy.com/

Chapter 23
Consensus Reality
Jenn Wertz

I sat on the veranda of my room in the golden red canyons of Sedona, dialing up a woman named Joy from a weekly newspaper ad. I was calling to book an energy healing session. The modality was a two-part process, Joy explained, said to align one with a "higher universal grid" and with one's higher path, in general. She would trace lines on my body the first day, and a few days later, she would ground this new grid into my energy field. Energy healing was not a new concept to me; I'd had Reiki sessions before and found them helpful and relaxing. I also collected crystals, practiced the Law of Attraction, and believed there was an imminent shift in human evolution on our collective horizon.

It was February of 1996, and I had traveled from Pittsburgh, Pennsylvania to Sedona, Arizona for a weeklong trip. I was just beginning what would end up being a four-year hiatus from touring and recording with my platinum-selling, tribal rock band, and I was ready to start a new chapter in life. My departure from the band had been a rocky one, and I'd heard that Sedona was a beautiful vortex location with lots of good energy. It seemed like a great place to jumpstart a new chapter.

Nothing extraordinary happened during that first energy session. Joy just traced lines onto my body, and I went on my way. An hour after the session, however, I began to feel an intense, tingly heat growing at the base of my skull. I noticed the colors had a shimmering, grid-like pattern to them as they danced across the red rocks. The heat proceeded to crawl up to my crown and back down my legs, causing an electrical vibration. It felt kind of "trippy," and I became uncomfortable.

I was anxious to complete the alignment, as Joy had assured me that it would all settle down once we "grounded it in." And I trusted that, because sometimes energy work can create a mild shift. But during the second session, I experienced the sensation of falling backward at high speed! I opened my eyes to grid lines against darkness, the room itself flickering in and out of being. *This is not mild,* I thought. I panicked.

That night I woke up sweating, seemingly elevated over my hotel bed, facing an infinite, writhing tunnel of light. For a moment, I wondered if I was dead. I wasn't. The golden tunnel eventually evaporated, but the intensified electrical buzzing now whipped up my spine. It would "traffic jam" at the base of my skull, causing my flesh to crawl all over. I ended up vomiting for hours, on and off.

Had I been drugged? Did I have food poisoning? Is this some kind of psychic attack?

I sat on the plane back to Pittsburgh, twitching and nauseous. I'd hoped that being back home would jolt me back to my old Self, but instead, panic attacks came in cascading succession. Swooshes of spiraling, electrical zaps traversed my whole body every waking second. It was terrifying but interspersed with contrasting episodes of overwhelming ecstasy. At times, I was certain that I was one with the very air around me and that if I closed my eyes, I would float out of my body and evaporate. The latter may sound lovely, but my mind was processing all of it as an assault. My fight-or-flight response triggered me into panic attacks and the occasional episode of paranoid thinking. It was an extraordinarily upsetting state of being. I stayed in bed for that entire first week.

It was during this time that a whole different type of extraordinary experience began. Every morning before dawn, I was awakened by those physical, electrical storms. The first time it happened, I was jolted awake. The electricity pulled itself up out of my spine and transformed into what looked like a laser-lined holographic show in my vision field. I was shown geometric formations that were glowing, animated, and morphing. It had an amusing, calming effect on me. It was as if the panicky electricity couldn't affect me physically while it was arranging itself into these mutating shapes.

Over weeks, these early morning shows evolved into scenes illustrating simultaneous existence. Time was shown to me as a cylindrical spiral moving upward rather than a chronological line. I was shown how we, as humans, traverse time in experiential reality, spiraling up in layers. But it is all happening in an eternal "now," divided into fields of experience.

There seemed to be a team of some type of guides presenting these pre-dawn "sessions." They were downloading into my mental awareness what felt akin to an instruction manual. If I had a new experience, I would learn more about that experience in the next early morning session. For instance, I noticed I was now able to see and feel things that emanated from people that I encountered. It was startling and confusing. This was soon addressed by the team. They showed me that this happens because fragmented energy is held in the outer layers of one's energy field, unless it's integrated. One example would be a person who is holding a repressed trauma experience. Because every human being is simultaneously a transmitter and receiver of energy, someone sensitive like me could walk by and pick up that fragmented energy, like a radio station. I would need to learn a process they called "energetic discernment" in order to *purposefully* choose what to engage or not engage with.

The early morning sessions eventually expanded into a dialogue. I didn't experience myself channeling. Rather, I would describe it as having a "sparkling conversation" with these guides. The communication had a decidedly humorous and even lovingly sarcastic slant to it but always with a fundamentally warm, patient, and benevolent tone. I initially understood the team working with me were higher Beings and perceived them as a council or roundtable. But I soon came to understand, at least on a superficial level, that *I* was also one of *them*—a higher, more advanced version of me was sitting at that table. We were a team.

I sought help from a broad-minded psychiatric doctor who, thankfully, diagnosed that I had not lost my connection with reality but rather, was connecting to an *expanded* experience of reality. She felt that anxiety medication could temporarily keep the panic at lower levels while I digested my experiences. Eventually, I may get back to *normal*, she said, but cautioned that would likely require an expansion of my definition of *normal*.

So I was different. Everything was different.

Four months into my experience, I was invited to meet with an advanced energy healer of national acclaim. He and his colleagues believed that what likely happened to me was called a *spontaneous kundalini awakening*. They cautioned me to be very mindful of what I consume . . . from food, to media, to films, to even human interaction. It was all a vibrational energetic exchange, they said. Until I developed these skills of discernment, I would need to be vigilant, or I could be easily overwhelmed. They helped me learn to hone my perception and develop that discernment. They also introduced me to the fact that, as electromagnetic Beings, grounding allows us to conduct the influx of energy without blowing a fuse. Grounding became essential for me.

The pre-dawn sessions with my team continued to expand. I was shown visceral holographic scenes depicting how souls move through the spiral of time. We master each position, or lifetime, and then move onto the next level, up into a different paradigm; then we explore that spectrum. These were shown to me as classrooms, within which, we do our soul's work. There are many layers of spectrums and paradigms to learn from.

While this information-downloading process was mentally manage-able, physically it caused great strain in my spine, sacrum, and cranial bones. My team illustrated that this was because the expansion of consciousness requires a greater flow of cerebral spinal fluid in the physical body to facilitate the increase in electromagnetic activity. Seeing a chiropractic applied kinesiologist regularly for adjustments helped to physically accommodate my continued expansion. Neuro-Emotional Technique (NET) and supportive supplements were also beneficial. After eighteen months, with these and other supports in place, I was able to stop using the anxiety medication.

One of the more mind-blowing concepts the team showed me had to do with multiple streams of realities that we can "tune" into. The *main* stream of reality that we are operating in is a system that my team calls the *consensus reality*—what the majority of people agree is real. This includes all the rules about what is possible, as well as all the limitations. We can choose to *tune out* of one reality and *tune in* to another, simply by changing our frequency.

By late 1999, I was living in the mountains of Asheville, North Carolina, where things had gotten back to a new kind of normal. But I was exhausted. A girl can get tired of having to be vigilant about everything all the time! I felt blessed to receive all the lessons and information, I really did, but I was still so overwhelmed. I just wasn't ready to process it all yet. I felt isolated and disillusioned.

When the year 2000 arrived, almost exactly four years after my trip to Sedona, I packed up my crystals and books and put them in a big box. I also "boxed up" my hopes and beliefs about a big collective shift in human consciousness. I developed the attitude that I'd been duped, somehow . . . that spiritual work is dangerous and out of control. There was surely no divine force guiding me, let alone guiding humanity to some planet-wide shift! I felt victimized by the entire experience and wanted to retreat under the *veil* that had spontaneously lifted from me in Sedona.

It wasn't hard to go back "to sleep." I moved from the idyllic mountains back to dear old Pittsburgh. I learned that alcohol, television, cigarettes, and playing in trauma-dramas beautifully buffered my sensitivity, shrouding me, once again, behind the veil. Thank God for vices! Within months of my willful descent back into the *consensus reality*, I was invited to reunite with the band, to tour and record. Imagine that! It was an exciting and fun way to keep everything in line with what I remembered as my *normal*.

For the next twenty years, it worked . . . keeping me cynical and safe, buffered from the sparkling and untethered truth. I had a beautiful son, left the band again, and started making art. Over the years, little things would poke through the veil, but I didn't have any space for that. I had tour dates and parent-teacher conferences to attend! I anchored myself into what could pass for a mostly joyful, albeit slightly cynical and messy, *normal* life.

I stayed in that holding pattern right up until the spring of 2020. During the global silence of quarantine, I was suddenly prompted, by a swooning familiarity, to lie down. It was non-negotiable.

And just like that, they were back. There was no panic or electrical discomfort this time. Within the swoon of energy, the connection to my team returned, in seamless continuity with the last communication from twenty years earlier. The tone and feeling were the same, the affectionately firm, salty humor intact. They picked back up with,

"As we were saying . . . ," as if no time had passed. After all, for them, none had.

They showed me that humanity *was* moving into a higher band-width, bringing with it, a new paradigm. Our reality would be getting an upgrade, they said. This would be a very exciting time, for sure, but also a trying time for many, because the shift to higher conscious-ness requires the integration of fragmented, lower-density energies, both individually and collectively. This integration of polarities will play out on the world stage, as well as in our personal lives over the next several years. Anything that doesn't match the new, higher frequencies will come up to be seen, felt, and ultimately, integrated.

The dialogue with my team in this grounded re-awakening felt different—the information was somehow familiar, a kind of déjà vu of dormant knowledge. Much of what I used to experience as *down-loads,* I now understood as spontaneous *remembrances* that continued to unfold over days, weeks, or months.

Since 2020, I've had many fascinating remembrances of my "past" lives or dimensional experiences, along with an expanded compre-hension of sacred geometry, sound frequencies, and the human energy body and electromagnetic field. I've been shown that I am only one of millions of human beings that are here at this time, anchoring new frequencies into our collective field, literally laying the groundwork for the new paradigm. Some people are aware they are doing it, some aren't. Either way, these anchor points create an *etheric grid,* or network, across the earth that will eventually manifest in our reality as higher consciousness. The new humans, being born now, are already equipped with the corresponding, upgraded frequencies.

I now have the understanding that I was anchoring these frequency points as early as my childhood, in the 1980s, as well as during the 1990s, while I traveled the world as a rock musician. Remember that twenty-year holding pattern during which I thought I went back to sleep? Yes . . . I was anchoring even then. We are connected to our higher path, whether we are consciously aware of it or not . . . whether we are in what we understand as a "divine flow" or what feels like a dormant, disconnected time.

Some may deem my experience a far-out, singular oddity, reserved only for "other people." On the contrary, I've been shown that this type of spiritual connection is not only available to every human being but is at play in all our lives, all the time. We all have higher consciousness—people simply have different degrees of awareness of it. In my work, I have learned that everyday people experience expanded states quite often but may not share them with others out of fear of ridicule.

Staying grounded and present in our human experience is cardinal within the ebb and flow of awakening, which can create painful cognitive dissonance at times. The *consensus reality* can seem unreal, backwards, and bizarre. We might be confronted with our outgrown tribal identity systems, losing our connection to things that are no longer aligned with our authentic selves. We may seek to return to the comfort of our old identities, only to find that they're not available. We not only outgrew them; they aren't even on our frequency anymore—we are tuning into a completely different radio station. Be assured, however . . . we can process our grief over the loss of our outgrown parts and eventually find our grounding in the new levels.

It's also easy to get caught up on the human hamster wheel of striving and achieving. But even in mid spin, we can maintain a glimpse of the truth. The truth of ourselves as miraculous physical manifestations of vibrational energy. The truth that our worth is not measured by our productivity or defined by what we achieve. We still must pay the bills and keep schedules, but when we really know our worth is inherent as creations of divine Source, we begin to effortlessly strive toward a more authentic expression of ourselves. A critical mass is reached; once we see that expanded reality, we can't un-see it, because consciousness evolution is an autonomic system that naturally strives upward, magnetically gravitating toward a higher-dimensional reality, once encountered.

Like all of us, I have downturns and days in my human experience where I want to scream. But through my journey I've become aware of a *divine tapestry* weaving throughout my life, and lifetimes, in a perfect fractal unfolding. I cannot begin to fathom the workings of it. But I have seen it. And there are times that the simple awareness of it brings me ecstatic joy and true understanding. Additionally, while navigating hard terrain and shifts in this reality, the awareness of this tapestry brings me great comfort in my concern for myself, my loved ones, and for our collective. This awareness is one of the greatest gifts of my life.

Not long after my reawakening, my path led me to Quantum Healing —the modalities of Beyond Quantum Healing (BQH) and Quantum Connect (QC) instantly resonated with me. I soon integrated those modalities, as well as Shamanic Soul Retrieval, into my practice. The divine tapestry is consistently clever. It transformed my traumatic awakening experiences into the touchstone of my work as a practitioner. I now use the very skills that I was forced to develop, back then, in my healing work with folks entering their own awakening journeys.

Today, in addition to my Quantum Healing practice, I am writing two books, adjusting to empty nesting, and making art. The crux of my personal work is continuing to learn the integration of expanded states, which is more real and normal to me now than anything else.

Jenn Wertz is a Quantum Healer, musician, songwriter, and artist best known as an original member of Rusted Root, a multi-platinum, tribal rock band started in 1990 in Pittsburgh, Pennsylvania. The band's 1994 release "When I Woke" (Island Def Jam) is a multiplatinum, full-length album featuring the hit *Send Me on My Way*, which has been featured in many major films, television shows, and commercials.

Rusted Root, known for their high energy live shows, toured for many years to sold out crowds across North America, sharing billing with classic acts like The Allman Brothers Band, The Grateful Dead, Santana, Page and Plant, and the Dave Matthews Band, among others.

Wertz left the band for four and a half years in mid-1995, reuniting with them in early 2000. After many more years of touring and recording, Jenn left the band for good in 2007 and settled into being mom to her son. Her continuing creative impulse led her to create mixed-media visual art, which has been featured as the backdrop of a ballet, a book cover, and in various art exhibitions throughout Pittsburgh since 2009.

"I stay healthy by staying creative," says Wertz. "It's my meditation. If I'm not working on something, I lose my emotional and spiritual grounding."

In 2020, during the worldwide pandemic, Wertz experienced a dramatic reconnection with her spiritual path, that led her to become a certified Quantum Healer in the Beyond Quantum Healing modality, integrating Reiki and sound into her vibrational healing sessions. In 2022, she added Shamanic Soul Retrieval, a form of past and current life integration, to her practice, Quantum Healing Pittsburgh.

Wertz currently lives, makes art, and practices Quantum Healing in Pittsburgh, Pennsylvania. She is currently writing both a memoir and a nonfiction book.

Learn more about Jenn at www.jennwertz.com

For general inquiries/contact: askjennwertz@gmail.com

Glossary

Angels: Spiritual beings, often depicted as beings of light or energy, believed to act as messengers, protectors, or guides between the divine and the human realm.

Akashic Records: A metaphysical concept referring to a compendium of universal events, thoughts, and emotions, accessible through spiritual practices.

Awakening: A process of spiritual realization or heightened awareness, often associated with personal transformation.

Beyond Quantum Healing (BQH): An advanced form of hypnosis, developed by Candace Craw-Goldman, that facilitates deep states of relaxation and altered consciousness, allowing individuals to access their higher self, explore past lives, and gain insights into their current life challenges.

Channeling: The process of receiving information or guidance from non-physical entities or energies through a conscious or semi-conscious state.

Chakra: Energy centers in the human body, according to Eastern traditions, believed to regulate emotional and physical well-being.

Chod: A Tibetan Buddhist practice involving ritual chanting and visualization to cut through ego and attachment.

Craniosacral Therapy: A gentle, light touch healing modality that focuses on the craniosacral system, which includes the membranes and fluid surrounding the brain and spinal cord.

Discarnate: A being or spirit that exists without a physical body, often believed to communicate through mediums.

Dolores Cannon: A hypnotherapist and author known for pioneering *Quantum Healing Hypnosis Technique* (QHHT®) and work in past-life regression.

Duality (Non-Duality): The philosophical concept of opposites (such as good and evil, light and dark) and the transcendence of these dualities to experience oneness.

Empath: A person with a heightened ability to sense and absorb the emotions, energies, or mental states of others, often experiencing them as if they were their own.

Energetic Attachments: Invisible entities or energies that attach to individuals, potentially influencing their emotions or behavior.

Energy: Energy refers to the vital life force or subtle essence that permeates all living beings and the universe.

Energy Medicine: A holistic healing approach that focuses on manipulating the body's subtle energy fields to promote physical, emotional, and spiritual well-being.

Entities: Spiritual beings or intelligences, which can be positive, negative, or neutral, encountered through channeling, meditation, or altered states.

Eschatology: A branch of theology concerned with the end of the world, death, and the ultimate destiny of humanity.

Equid: A member of the family *Equidae*, which includes hoofed mammals, such as horses, donkeys, and zebras.

Frequency: The vibrational rate at which energy moves through the body or the universe. It is believed that different emotions, thoughts, and physical states correspond to specific frequencies.

Galactic: Relating to a galaxy, especially the Milky Way, or involving phenomena, objects, or systems within or pertaining to galaxies.

God: The transcendent, supreme being or divine force/source often regarded as the creator and sustainer of the universe.

Grounding: A practice or concept involving connection to the Earth, either physically or mentally, to promote emotional stability, well-being, or electrical balance.

Healing Modalities: Various approaches and techniques used to promote physical, emotional, and spiritual well-being, encompassing a wide range of practices.

Higher Self: The aspect of a person's consciousness that transcends the ego and connects with universal wisdom.

Holistic: An approach to healing and well-being that considers the whole person—mind, body, and spirit—emphasizing the interconnectedness of all aspects of life and seeking balance across physical, emotional, mental, and spiritual health.

"Inner Work": The practice of self-reflection and psychological or spiritual development aimed at personal growth.

Intuitive: Referring to the natural ability to understand or know something without the need for conscious reasoning or analysis.

Kundalini: A form of divine energy believed to lie dormant at the base of the spine, often awakened through yoga or meditation.

Law of Attraction: A belief that positive or negative thoughts bring corresponding experiences into a person's life through the power of intention.

Life Coach: A professional who assists individuals in identifying and achieving personal and professional goals by providing guidance, support, and accountability and using various techniques, including motivational interviewing and goal-setting strategies, to help clients enhance self-awareness, overcome obstacles, and create actionable plans for improvement in various areas of life.

Loosh: A term popularized by Robert Monroe, referring to energy generated by human emotions, often seen as food for non-physical entities.

Mantra Meditation: A form of meditation where repetitive chanting of a phrase or sound is used to calm the mind and cultivate focus. *See also* Meditation.

Meditation: A practice involving mental focus, mindfulness, or contemplation to achieve spiritual awareness or relaxation.

Metaphysics: A branch of philosophy that explores the fundamental nature of reality, existence, and the relationship between mind and matter.

Near-Death Experience (NDE): A profound psychological or spiritual experience reported by individuals who have come close to death or experienced clinical death and were subsequently revived.

Neuro-Linguistic Programming (NLP): A psychological approach that uses language patterns and techniques to influence thought patterns and behavior.

New Earth: A vision of a higher-dimensional world characterized by spiritual awakening and collective consciousness.

OBE (Out-of-Body Experience): A phenomenon where a person feels as though their consciousness is separated from their physical body, often during sleep or meditation.

Parapsychology: The study of phenomena that lie outside the scope of traditional scientific understanding, such as telepathy, clairvoyance, psychokinesis, and near-death experiences, often focusing on the exploration of the mind's potential beyond known physical laws.

Past Life Regression (QHHT®, BQH): A therapeutic technique that uses hypnosis to access memories from previous lifetimes.

- **QHHT®**: *Quantum Healing Hypnosis Technique*, developed by Dolores Cannon, focusing on past-life exploration and healing.
- **BQH**: *Beyond Quantum Healing*, a modern adaptation of QHHT®, developed by Candace Craw-Goldman, that allows remote sessions.

Pleiadians: A race of extraterrestrial beings who originated from the star cluster Pleiades.

Portal: In a spiritual context, a portal refers to a gateway or opening that facilitates a connection between different dimensions, realms, or states of consciousness.

Post-Traumatic Stress Disorder (PTSD): A mental health condition triggered by witnessing or experiencing traumatic events.

Psychic: Relating to the ability to perceive information beyond the normal human senses, often considered a form of extrasensory perception (ESP).

Quantum Healing Hypnosis Technique (QHHT®): A hypnosis method developed by Dolores Cannon that guides individuals into a deep trance state, allowing access to the subconscious or higher self.

Quantum Physics: A branch of physics that explores the behavior of matter and energy at the smallest scales, where particles can exist in multiple states simultaneously and are interconnected beyond classical understanding.

Reality: The state of things as they exist.

Reiki: A Japanese healing practice involving energy transfer through the hands to promote relaxation and healing.

Shadow (Shadow Work): The process of identifying and integrating unconscious aspects of the self that have been repressed or denied.

Shamanism: A spiritual practice involving a practitioner (shaman) interacting with the spirit world to promote healing or insight.

Somatic: Relating to the body, especially in the context of therapies that address physical sensations to process emotional experiences.

Source: In spiritual contexts, "Source" refers to the origin of all creation, often described as the ultimate, infinite energy or consciousness that underlies and connects everything in existence.

Spirit Guides: Non-physical entities, thought to operate from a higher spiritual realm and taking many forms, including ancestors, animal spirits, ascended masters, or other benevolent beings, believed to offer guidance, support, and wisdom to individuals throughout their life journey.

Starseed: A person believed to have originated from other dimensions or planets to assist humanity in spiritual growth and transformation.

Tarot: A divination tool consisting of a deck of seventy-eight cards, each with unique imagery, symbolism, and meanings.

Toning: The practice of using vocal sounds to create healing vibrations and harmonize the body and mind.

Trauma-Informed Yoga: A therapeutic approach to yoga that acknowledges the impact of trauma on individuals and incorporates principles of safety, empowerment, and sensitivity to promote healing and self-awareness.

Vagus Nerve: A key nerve in the parasympathetic nervous system, involved in regulating heart rate, digestion, and emotional responses.

Index

A

Abraham (channeled entity), 39, 178. *See also* Hicks, Esther

Abrahamic religions, ix

Acupressure, 159. *See also* Healing Modalities

Acupuncture, 77, 78,132. *See also* Healing Modalities

Afrikaans, 169

Akashic Records, 26, 151, 156. *See also* Glossary *and* Healing Modalities

Alcoholics Anonymous (AA), 213, 214

Aldebaran, 226

Alexander, Dr. Eben, 132

Anderson, Robert, MD, 45

Angels, 35, 120, 148-156,192, 210, 214. *See also* Glossary

Animal Empath, 60. *See also* Spiritual Gifts

Appalachian Mountains, Appalachian Trail, 16-18, 160, 161

Apocalypse, ix, x

Arizona, Sedona, 228-9, 234

Arroyo, Stephen, 158

Astrology, Karma and Transformation, 158

Atlantis, 50

Arkansas, 59

Arthur Findlay College, 174, 176

Awaken the Spirit Within, 132

Awakening, *See* Glossary

B

Baptist, 88, 89, 90, 94

Beyond Quantum Healing (BQH), 81, 104, 152, 162, 165, 173, 176, 177, 185, 191, 205, 208, 228, 237, 338. *See also* Glossary *and* Healing Modalities

Bible, The:

  Adam, 138-9

  Elijah, 89

Acknowledgments

This anthology would not have been possible without my soul-mate and publishing partner, Will, who was instrumental in not only the gorgeous cover design but also the interior formatting. Beyond just this project, however, his unwavering love and support provide me with the freedom to create.

I am incredibly grateful to each of our twenty-three amazing authors and humbled by their trust: in Will and me, in the process, and in themselves. These selfless souls, with a desire to be of service to our readers, often overcame great trepidation. Some felt they were not strong writers; others were apprehensive about sharing their deeply personal experiences. I thank each of them for the beautiful story they have gifted the world.

Many thanks to lead author and cherished friend, Judy Buchanan, for her support and logistical assistance on this project.

Immense gratitude to Julie Sivell, who served as the developmental editor, helping our authors birth their beautiful stories. Her compassion, encouragement, and professional guidance was a blessing to all.

A special thanks to our early endorsers for the gift of their time and for their kind words of support: Paul Chek, Blossom Goodchild, Michiko Hayashi, Cynthia Sue Larson, Debra Moffitt, Anita Moorjani, and Emmy Vadnais.

Thank you to Donna Kennedy, my friend and cheerleader, for her assistance with the proofreading process.

Last, but certainly not least, I give great thanks to my guides and helpers across the veil for their inspiration and divine guidance.

About the Editor

Dr. Allison Brown is an award-winning author, educator, and quantum healer. As a full-time public school counselor, Allison holds a master's degree in counseling psychology and a doctorate in educational leadership. In 2014 her search for reconciliation between a newfound spirituality and her traditional Christian upbringing led her on an amazing journey of self-discovery. In her role as a Reiki Master teacher and Beyond Quantum Healing practitioner, Allison uses a unique blend of metaphysical practices and counseling technique to assist clients.

Allison's books include *The Origin Story: Rediscovering Our Galactic Ancestors, Love Notes from the Animal Kingdom,* and *The Journey Within: A Christian's Guide to 14 Non-traditional Spiritual Practices.* Allison was also a co-author of the Amazon best-seller, *The Ancestor's Within: Reveal and Heal the Ancient Memories You Carry.* This anthology, *Awakening Stories,* is her editorial debut.

Allison and her husband, Will, co-founded Palm and Lotus, LLC, which serves as an umbrella for their many activities, including their metaphysical work, The Treehouse event space in Moncks Corner, South Carolina, and their independent publishing house, Palm and Lotus Publishing. Will and Allison are co-hosts, along with their friend, Samantha Kaufman, of the *Out on a Limb* podcast, a platform on which they engage in entertaining, metaphysical discussions, as well as enlightened conversations with unique, spiritually-minded guests.

To learn more about Allison, Will, and their work, please visit the following sites:

https://drallisonbrown.com/

https://www.facebook.com/drallibrown

https://www.quantumhealers.com/drallisonbrown

https://palmandlotus.com/

About Palm & Lotus Publishing

Palm and Lotus is an independent, boutique publisher whose mission is to provide a professional and personalized experience to authors seeking a platform in the area of spirituality and consciousness exploration. Because we understand that the publishing process can be intimidating, expensive, and time consuming, our nurturing environment is particularly advantageous for first-time authors. Our goal at Palm and Lotus Publishing is to help authors create a stunning book at minimal cost, while allowing them to retain creative control over their work.

To learn more, visit:

https://palmandlotus.com/palm-and-lotus-publishing/

Other Titles by Palm & Lotus Publishing

The Origin Story: Rediscovering Our Galactic Ancestors

The Origin Story Companion Workbook

Love Notes from the Animal Kingdom

The Journey Within: A Christian's Guide to 14 Non-traditional Spiritual Practices

Anxiety is No Fun! A Holistic Approach to Overcome It

Journaling Workbook For Self-Care

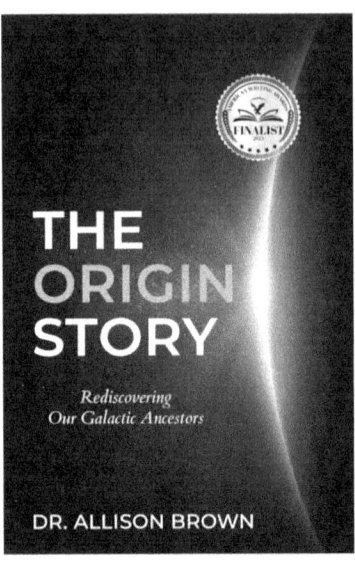

THE
ORIGIN
STORY

*Rediscovering
Our Galactic Ancestors*

DR. ALLISON BROWN

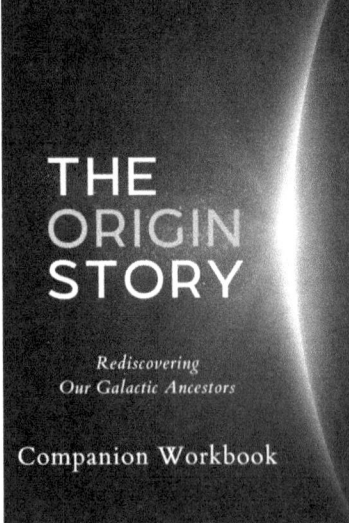

THE
ORIGIN
STORY

*Rediscovering
Our Galactic Ancestors*

Companion Workbook

LOVE
NOTES
FROM THE
ANIMAL
KINGDOM

DR. ALLISON BROWN

THE JOURNEY
A CHRISTIAN'S GUIDE TO
14 NON-TRADITIONAL
SPIRITUAL PRACTICES
WITHIN

DR. ALLISON BROWN

www.ingramcontent.com/pod-product-compliance
Lightning Source LLC
Chambersburg PA
CBHW060905120626
46553CB00001B/210